WO
AS LEADERS:
STRATEGIES FOR EMPOWERMENT
&
COMMUNICATION

Edited by Linda Ellis Eastman

Professional Woman Publishing
Prospect, Kentucky

WOMEN AS LEADERS: STRATEGIES FOR EMPOWERMENT
& COMMUNICATION
Copyright © 2007 by Linda Ellis Eastman
All rights reserved.

Published by:
Professional Woman Publishing
Post Office Box 333
Prospect, KY 40059
(502) 228-0906
http://www.prowoman.net

Please contact the publisher for quantity discounts.

ISBN 13: 978-0-9799711-0-5
ISBN 10: 0-9799711-0-1

Library of Congress Cataloging-In-Publication Data

Cover Design and Typography by:
Sential Design, LLC — www.sentialdesign.com

Printed in the United States of America

Dedicated to Julia Owen Schap,
a gifted musician and magnificent friend.

TABLE OF CONTENTS

TABLE OF CONTENTS
-CONTINUED-

TABLE OF CONTENTS
-CONTINUED-

ABOUT THE AUTHOR

LINDA EASTMAN

Linda Ellis Eastman is President and CEO of The Professional Woman Network (PWN), an International Training and Consulting Organization on Women's Issues. She has designed seminars which have been presented in China, the former Soviet Union, South Africa, the Phillipines, and attended by individuals in the United States from such firms as McDonalds, USA Today, Siemens-Westinghouse, the Pentagon, the Department of Defense, and the United States Department of Education.

An expert on women's issues, Ms. Eastman has certified and trained over one thousand women to start consulting/seminar businesses originating from such countries as Pakistan, the Ukraine, Antigua, Canada, Mexico, Zimbabwe, Nigeria, Bermuda, Jamaica, Costa Rica, England, South Africa, Malaysia, and Kenya. Founded in 1982 by Linda Ellis Eastman, The Professional Woman Network is committed to educating women on a global basis regarding, self-esteem, confidence building, stress management, and emotional, mental, spiritual and physical wellness.

Ms. Eastman has been featured in USA Today and listed in Who's Who of American Women, as well as Who's Who of International Leaders. In addition to women's issues, Ms. Eastman speaks internationally regarding the importance of human respect as it relates to race, color, culture, age, and gender. She will be facilitating an international conference where speakers and participants from many nations will be able to discuss issues that are unique to women on a global basis.

Linda Ellis Eastman is also founder of The Professional Woman Speakers Bureau and The Professional Woman Coaching Institute. Ms. Eastman has dedicated her businesses to increasing the self-esteem and personal dignity of women and youth around the world.

Contact
The Professional Woman Network
P.O. Box 333
Prospect, KY 40059
(502) 566-9900
lindaeastman@prodigy.net
www.prowoman.net
www.protrain.net

INTRODUCTION

Linda Ellis Eastman

Do women make excellent leaders? My personal feeling is that women have extraordinary and inherent skills which lend themselves to preparing women for leadership roles. Listening, sharing, empathy, teamwork, and communication are several of the skills that come to mind.

When you consider women managing homes, families, businesses, multi-tasking with aging parents, balancing home and work, serving on school and church committees, and standing up for their values, I believe the answer is found that yes, women can lead, for sure.

But what obstacles stand in the way of a woman leading? One of the greatest roadblocks is the woman herself. Women are altruistic by nature and are generally taking care of others and their needs much more so than their very own. Women may simply become their own worst enemy. Rather than slowing down, taking time to relax, reflect and schedule quality "ME" time, they oftentimes are racing around helping others.

This book is dedicated to the premise that women are (or can be) sensational leaders. The chapters bring insight into the challenges women may face while providing guidelines, tips, and support on a woman's journey to a leadership position.

The authors of this book have written insightful chapters that will provide women with the resources to face many of life's challenges with more conviction, strength, and a charted plan.

This book is for women of every age to encourage them to step up and stand up for what they believe is right, fair, honest, kind, inclusive, and respectful. Women have every right to take the lead and are incredibly talented and prepared to do so. May the writings of this book provide the courage to always stay the course.

WOMEN
AS LEADERS:
STRATEGIES FOR EMPOWERMENT
&
COMMUNICATION

ABOUT THE AUTHOR

PHYLLIS S. QUINLAN

Phyllis S. Quinlan resides in Flushing, New York. She has over 30 years experience in the healthcare industry with 25 years at a management level in emergency services, acute care and long term care/ short-term rehabilitation settings. Phyllis is also a consulting Feng Shui Practitioner and has practiced this complimentary therapy since 1999. She is presently pursuing her Doctorate Degree in Healthcare Administration at the Kennedy-Western University.

Phyllis is the president of MFW Consultants To Professionals, a Consulting Firm serving the educational, personal coaching, and managerial needs of individuals and organizations. As a certified legal nurse consult, she also serves as an expert witness to many attorney-clients.

Phyllis is a contributing author for the following PWN publications: *Overcoming the Superwoman Syndrome, Your on Stage: Image, Etiquette, Branding, and Style, Woman's Journey to Wellness: Body, Mind and Spirit* and *A Woman's Survival Guide to Overcoming Obstacles, Transition and Change.* As member of the PWN International Speakers Bureau, she is available internationally to assist the individual client and/or organization with professional development needs.

Phyllis' most cherished role is that of godmother to five fabulous young women. She wants to dedicate this chapter to each of them: Nicole M., Anita W., Alison F., Valerie F., and Emily B.

Contact:
Phyllis Quinlan, RNC, MS, CEN CCRN, CLNC
MFW Consultants To Professionals, Inc
147-20 35th Avenue #2B
Flushing, New York 11354
718 661 4981
mfwconsultants@mindspring.com
www.protrain.net

ONE

LIVING YOUR LIFE WITH COURAGE

By Phyllis S. Quinlan

As I look back at myself as a teenager and young adult, I am grateful for spending my most formative years surrounded by fabulous female role models at home, in school, and in the world. The women from each of these venues had a profound influence on me as I struggled to have a clear vision of who I was and how I could contribute meaningfully to the world. My list of heroines was remarkably diverse. They were feminists, stay-at-home moms, teachers, artists, political, and even religious figures. Each shared one incredible uncommon virtue. They lived their lives with courage.

Their individual forms of courage were as diverse as the group itself. They had the courage of their convictions, of faith, of vision, and the courage to protest injustice and demand true respect for themselves and other women. They challenged everything. Not just for the sake of challenge, but also for what they knew to be necessary, right, and long overdo. They did this with such apparent ease and confidence that no twenty-something could ever suspect the price that living your life with courage demands. Some thirty years later, I am only beginning to understand their achievement.

Compromise

Challenging authority, questioning conventional thinking, and championing causes are vital activities that serve to shape our ideals and beliefs as we transition from a youth to an adult.

Holding on to those ideals and beliefs and calling on them to guide our adult choices is not easy. Adult life introduces a whole new concept, the concept of compromise. Compromise can act like a sculptor's chisel working slowly on marble. Compromise chips away at you so that you are able to reshape yourself to fit into the reality of an adult world. But a word of caution, *too much compromise* can bring about a day when you no longer recognize yourself or know what you stand for. Living your life with courage can help ensure that you never see that dark day.

Develop Your Two Great Gifts

Adult life is all about choices. Many of our adult choices are clear and somewhat effortless. However, the choices that are the most challenging usually turn out to be the ones that impact our lives the greatest. How do you recognize these life-changing choices and find the right answer? You rely on a woman's two great gifts: intuition and emotion. Intuition is an internal sense of knowing. Emotions reflect our sense of balance. When faced with a decision, we absolutely need to develop the habit of checking in with ourselves.

What is your intuition telling you?

- Jump at the golden opportunity.

- Slow down and weigh your options.

- This choice is the easy way out of a tough situation

- You will be paying for this choice the rest of your life.

- This choice is tough, but the right thing to do.

What emotion is this choice bringing up?

- A welcomed sense of challenge and excitement

- Disturbing uncertainty

- A sense of guilt, or possibly shame

- Agony

- Gratitude

Taking the time necessary to check in and sort through your intuition and emotions can give you clarity on just how much compromise is entailed in making this choice. Choices that are aligned with your beliefs and ideals often present themselves as effortless decisions. Choices that compromise your sense of self and integrity are usually struggles to the end. Clearly, being honest with yourself is key to being able to utilize these two great gifts to the fullest. Being honest with yourself takes courage.

The Courage to Know Yourself and Resist Rationalizing

I do not think that there is one moment when you realize that you know yourself well. Truly knowing yourself is a process. Life continuously reshapes and redefines you as you work through the many roles and experiences on your path. It is important to understand that many of life's circumstances present themselves so that we can have the opportunity to know ourselves better and to test our personal courage. Celebrate those times when you have triumphed over your shortcomings. Hold yourself accountable for your mistakes, and learn from them.

Everyone rationalizes a decision. However, it is important to monitor how often you use this popular coping mechanism and how you feel when you use it. Rationalization can help you arrive at a choice that justifies incorrect behavior. It can help to explain away the sense that you are lying to yourself, and that your choice is not aligned with the message your intuition and emotions are trying to convey to you. It is important to acknowledge that this coping mechanism has the tendency to make you less honest with yourself, and dilute your personal courage when it is utilized excessively.

Nurturing the Courage in Your Character

I believe that each of us is born with an innate fortitude that once cultivated by loving, supportive siblings, friends, parents and adult's role models can mature into personal courage. However at some point you will need to rely on yourself to find and nurture the courage you will need throughout your life.

Choices often become more difficult as we grow older. Our roles and responsibilities expand. Family, friends, and professional colleagues rely on us. Sometimes it seems impossible to fulfill your responsibilities and remain true to yourself. It is at these moments that it is important to remember that courage is the bridge between your responsibility and your truth. Only you will know when a choice is not in alignment with your intuition and emotions. Only you will know that, no matter how something is repackaged or restated, that it is still wrong, and something you cannot do or support. Only you will know the price that you will need to pay for being courageous. How do you prepare yourself for such defining moments? I recommend incorporating routines into your life that can enrich and strengthen the quality of your character each and every day. Practicing these routines can help to ensure that when courage is called for, you will be ready.

1. Try your hardest to always be truthful. White lies are an adult world rationalization.

2. Live your life actively. Don't wait for life to happen to you. Go out there and make your life happen. Know that you are the creator of your life. Find the passion in your life. It will act like fuel to move you along your path.

3. Keep informed. Do not let any one person shape your viewpoint. Learn about the three sides of the personal, professional, and social issues in your life so you can make thoughtful choices. Understanding an issue to the best of your ability is the only way to truly have an informed opinion that you can discuss intelligently without becoming defensive.

4. Practice positive talk. Lord knows that there are volumes of negative messages out there greeting you on a daily basis. Recognize that

there are billion dollar industries that rely on techniques that encourage you to question yourself, so they can sell you the remedy for happiness.

5. Claim your joy. Make time for fun. Remember how to play. Develop your sense of humor. Laugh often.

6. Join in. Find the social or professional group that fits your needs and dreams. Then, become active in that group. Remember you must give in order to receive.

7. Read about courageous women. Their biographies are truly inspiring.

8. Explore the complimentary approaches to health and wellbeing. Limit the clutter in your environment. It can deplete your ability to think and see clearly. Keep color and music in your life. Consider making a monthly massage as necessary to maintaining your health as getting your flu vaccine.

9. Honor the principles of Feng Shui so that you can find your harmony and maintain your vibration in alignment with the Universe. Meditate. Pray to the Universe for the Grace you will need to meet life's challenges.

10. Don't confuse strength with courage. Stubbornness and an inability to be flexible are often mistaken for strength. Courage allows you to reconsider your viewpoint based on an increased understanding of the subject, and change your mind.

11. Surround yourself with people who are smarter or stronger than you. This takes more than a bit of courage, for it can be a humbling experience. Treat this experience as if you are sitting in a wonderfully

dynamic classroom. Breathe in the wisdom and the virtues. Quietly honor the wisdom and virtues of your teachers, and they will find their way into your being in a gradual, subtle way.

12. Keep hope alive in your life. Courage is about acting for the future. Courage is hope in action

Each generation of women will have their issues, choices, and defining moments. Whatever your challenges are, face them with courage.

References, and for Further Reading

1.   http://www.feminist.com/resources/artspeech/genwom/celebrate.htm

2.   http://www.greatwomen.org/

3.   http://scriptorium.lib.duke.edu/collections/african-american-women.html

4.   http://www.distinguishedwomen.com/index.html

5.   http://www.legacy98.org/timeline.html

ABOUT THE AUTHOR

MICKI K. JORDAN, MLDR

Micki Kremenak Jordan is a mentor, trainer and coach. She has held a variety of corporate management positions over the past 25 years. She has participated on Visioning and Strategic Planning Teams, Leadership Teams and in Training and Development of staff.

Micki has a Bachelor of Science Degree in Sociology from the University of Iowa. After several years in the corporate world she obtained her Masters of Arts in Leadership from Bellevue University, Bellevue, NE. Micki is certified in Diversity Training, Public Speaking and Professional Coaching and holds the Certified Insurance Councilor Designation. She is a member of the Professional Woman Network (PWN) serving on their International Advisory Board and the National Association of Female Executives (NAFE).

Her passion is assisting others to recognize their true potential. She has written chapters entitled "Living Your Values" and "Mirror Image", that may be found in the PWN publications *"Women's Survival Guide for Overcoming Obstacles, Transition and Change"* and *"Women's Journey to Wellness: Mind, Body & Spirit."* She also has a chapter entitled "Super Vision" in the book *"Overcoming the Superwoman Syndrome"*. All books are part of the PWN library.

Micki's plans for the future include developing and presenting small group seminars for college students and upwardly mobile career women as well as individual coaching. She also plans more writing.

Contact
Micki K. Jordan
863 Gleamstar Ave.
Las Vegas, NV 89123
(702) 463-5786
mickijordan@yahoo.com

TWO

ARE YOU A SHADOW OR A LIGHT?

By Micki K. Jordan

I have a little shadow that goes in and out with me,
And what can be the use of him is more than I can see.
He is very, very like me from the heels up to the head;
And I see him jump before me, when I jump into my bed.
From **A Child's Garden of Verses** *—Robert Louis Stevenson*

As a small child, I was fascinated with the discovery of my shadow. I watched it move as I directed. I could make it dance and jump and do almost any move I wanted it to perform as it followed my every action. Depending on the angle and amount of light, I could make it grow or shrink. It would change directions as I changed my position to

11

the light source that created the shadow. As I grew older, I learned how to make hand puppets on the wall. My friends and I would challenge each other to see who could be the most creative. As long as there was light, hours could be spent making and watching these shadows. Think about your younger days. Did you "play" with your shadow?

Being a shadow or being a light can be likened to Leadership Types. The shadow is someone who is reactive and controlling; the light personality is a creative and empowering person. To illustrate these traits, the following is a short parable about Shad and Sunny and their leadership styles.

Shad and Sunny are fraternal twins. Their physical appearance is as alike as it can be between a brother and a sister. Both are tall and slender, and move with an air of self-confidence. Graduates of a prestigious business school, they are hired by an International Marketing company. Each is placed in charge of a team of employees, and they are responsible for setting up trade shows across the country. Life is good.

As their careers progress, Shad and Sunny often find themselves working on the same projects. The results of their efforts, however, are very different. Shad's style of leading his team begins with establishing a plan, his plan. The individuals know exactly what is expected as he has told them many times exactly what HE expects each team member to do. There is little tolerance for any deviation. Shad is always looking for problems or issues, things that need be get fixed. He continually goes over the whole process in his mind and on paper. As far as he is concerned, the team functions like "a well oiled machine", every step and process done the same way every time. Shad is pleased with HIS plan and with the outcome of HIS work.

Sunny, on the other hand, calls a meeting before every project. She presents the information to her team members and calls for ideas.

Everyone is allowed to participate with ideas on how to achieve the needed end result. The tasks are assigned with everyone knowing what their part needs to do. Sunny watches the progress, asking questions and making observations. If she sees something going astray, she will quickly gather all the team members involved. They will brainstorm the solution, establishing any necessary changes, and then move forward. When the set-up is complete, the entire team will celebrate their latest creation. They are all satisfied with THEIR final product.

Shad's end result is becoming more predictable, always reflecting his personality and ideas. Sunny's team comes up with fresh new ideas for every show that reflect the customer and their product. Suddenly, Sunny and Shad's careers are moving at a different pace. Sunny and her team are in demand to create "magical presentations" for their customers. Shad is only in demand by those customers that want their product displayed in the same manner every time.

Who do you think would have the more requested team?_____

_____

Why? _____

What do you think are the differences in the leadership styles of Shad and Sunny?_____

_____

_____

Are they a shadow or a light? _____

As we look at the contrasts between these two types, consider your own style; determine where you might be, and then think about what you might need to do for self-development. Be honest with yourself as we examine aspects of each characteristic of being a shadow or a light.

Control

The shadow personality wants to be in complete control, and they are afraid of losing that control over others. They are the person that dictates tasks, assigning specific tasks to specific people. Strict limits are set on the guidelines given, with little or no deviations allowed. In a single word, this is micromanagement! The leader is always making sure everything works by a predetermined blue print. Dwight D. Eisenhower felt this style did not demonstrate true leadership. As he described it, *"You do not lead by hitting people over the head – that's assault, not leadership."*

The leader who would be considered a light knows results are achieved by relaxing controls. Guidelines are just a guide providing a fluid and flexible boundary. This is not to say people are allowed to take whatever action they choose. Instead, processes and desired outcomes are discussed among the individuals involved. Consensus is reached with periodic reviews, revealing any necessary tweaking or changes that are needed along the way. The goal is reached together with everyone gaining satisfaction from their contribution.

Shadow and Light leadership styles operate in a push me – pull you dichotomy, with the shadow mode continually pushing others for the leader's desired results, and the light pulling others toward their common vision and goals. The shadow's tendency is to focus on finding problems and fixing them. They are never satisfied, continually analyzing an issue, taking processes apart, recreating them and then telling others how to proceed. Their desire is to block the angle of the light, keeping the shadows behind them, following and imitating the leaders every move. Their subordinates begin to expect directions and being told their next steps. Often those that fail to perform in the intended way and to the expected level are pushed away.

The leaders that are providing light are **responsive** rather than **reactive.** They are aware of the situations around them and will focus on using strengths among the people to pull them toward the finish. They will encourage independent efforts. Subordinates and followers of the light learn the importance of self-responsibility. They learn to make decisions and to accept the consequences of their actions. They learn from the mistakes that are made and discover how to improve upon the desired results.

The secret to encouraging others is to get excited about the right things.
Some people get excited about pointing out mistakes,
or findings someone's failures. Instead, we should get excited about their
strengths and the little things they're doing right.
—John C. Maxwell

Communication

Communication is another area with dramatic differences between the shadow and light leadership types. Communication involves how a person gives and / or receives information from another person. The communication may be intentional or unintentional, and may be verbal or nonverbal in nature.

The shadow type of leader will tend to dominate a conversation. This relates to their need to control. They often will not allow the other party in the conversation time to finish their statements. The shadow will cut off a discussion if it is leading in a direction they do not want it to go. They are more on the giving end of information than on the receiving. Comments can tend to be far more cold and critical.

Communicating with a light type of leader is a pleasurable and uplifting experience. Their voice is enthusiastic. It communicates their feelings toward the other person, indicating friendliness, an appreciation of and an acceptance of the thoughts and ideas being presented. They will speak in an easily understood manner of speech, avoiding words and statements that might be confusing or condescending.

Listening is not one of the shadow's better skills. Since they want to be in control, they tend to over-analyze all situations; they want to have the final say in a conversation. They are usually busy thinking of the next comment they are going to make, the next thing they need to do, or are unwilling to accept someone else's opinion. They will tend to cut off a conversation, or cut into one with a comment without even really knowing what is being said. A conversation with a shadow person can become very frustrating and often one-sided. Usually, little is accomplished, other than the leader's position becomes more firmly implanted in the minds of others.

Individuals with the leadership style of being a light are usually excellent at communication. They have no desire to dominate a conversation. They are thoughtful in their speech, often asking questions to gain more clarity. They will use fewer words in order to reduce confusion. They feel they can learn from listening to what others have to say.

I remind myself every morning; nothing I say this day will teach me anything. So if I'm going to learn, I must do it by listening."—Larry King

The differences in types are easily demonstrated with their nonverbal communication. The shadow will appear to be restless. They will tend to allow their gaze to wander from the person they are conversing with. Their facial expressions will reveal their impatience, disagreement or displeasure. They are not good at hiding, nor do they try to hide their personal feelings. Facial expressions may include rolling eyes, a smirk, a grimace, or that "oh please!" look. There may actually be a failure by the shadow leader to pick up on what is NOT being said.

The light style will look at their co-communicator. They will make eye contact. Their face will show concentration and genuine interest in the subject.

They will occasionally use head movements to indicate agreement, or possibly a tilt of the head to acknowledge a statement they may want to question or comment on. There will be a neutral or friendly appearance to the light's face – it will almost "light up" with interest in what the speaker has to offer. They are observant of the body language and non-verbal actions of the person speaking. Light people are skilled in understanding the things that are not being said, but that are being communicated.

It is important to remember how people communicate their feelings and attitudes:

7 % comes through the spoken word.
38% are communicated by the tone of voice.
55% are by nonverbal signals.

Commitment

The final area we will consider is commitment to the leader and to tasks performed. Which type would you imagine would have the greater commitment both from their followers, and to them as well? There are some people that are very comfortable being in the shadow of others. These are individuals that may have low self-confidence or low self-esteem. A leader with the shadow tendency will capitalize on these people. They are easy to manipulate and mold into the robotic type of team members desired. The shadow type has no desire to assist or to lead the person into becoming anything other than the leader's shadow. To the leader, imitation is a form of flattery, and they are very flattered to have their every move and every idea imitated.

The light style leader thrives on providing the guiding light for their followers to be able to develop into future leaders. They are tuned into the motivation and make up of individuals creating the environment that allows others to thrive and grow. They will provide the ability for others to see the options available. They become the beacon to follow. The leader's light shines brightly as they watch the accomplishments of others, observing as their "followers" begin to provide and develop their own group of followers, thus stepping into leadership roles.

Review

As a review, look at the following chart and rank yourself on a scale of 0-10 for each trait listed:

Shadow		Light	
	Needs to have all of the answers		Doesn't need to have all the answers
	Tell oriented		Listen oriented
	Personally makes all of the decisions		Empowers others to make their own decisions
	Pushes for results		Pulls others toward goal or vision
	Over analyzes everything, and then will analyze more		Listens to intuition
	Creates sporadic motivation		Creates lasting commitments
	Very opinionated		Very open-minded
	Subordinates learn to expect direction		Teaches self-responsibility
	Always in a self-protect mode		Models self-responsibility
	Afraid of losing control		Relaxes controls to get results
	Focused on finding and fixing problems		Focused on building on individual strengths
	Quick to dismiss those that do not perform as desired		Teaches you can learn from your mistakes

Adapted from *Enlightened Leadership Theory,* by Sharon Bender

What have you discovered from the review of these traits? Are you more of a shadow or a light? Are there traits and tendencies you need to work on? Use the following space to list those things you wish to change in your leadership style, and some ideas of how you can accomplish these changes.

Trait #1 : _____

Change_____

Trait #2 : _____

Change_____

Trait #3 : _____

Change_____

I leave you with this final thought from John Maxwell. *"A candle's flame loses nothing when it lights another."* Become the style of leader that passes on that flame, creating the opportunity for others to develop themselves into their full potential, and creating future leaders.

Notes:

ABOUT THE AUTHOR

MARY FISCHER-MCKEE, PH.D.

Dr. Mary Fischer-McKee's experience has provided her with the opportunity to learn business and leadership from the ground up. From her early days of working as a door-to-door sales representative for AVON Cosmetics, through the start-up and ultimate sale of a family business, and through her current position as an executive for a Fortune 500 insurance company, Mary has been committed to women's issues in business and her local community.

Since 1999, her professional focus has been dedicated to developing products and services to help resolve the working uninsured crisis in the United States. As a knowledgeable resource in the insurance industry, Mary has provided educational and informational workshops and presentations to companies nationwide. As a committed member of her profession, Mary serves as an insurance industry ambassador to the local community by providing coaching and support to individuals for filing health insurance claims, appealing insurance company denials, and securing coverage.

As a member of the Professional Woman Network and the National Association of Female Executives, Mary passionately supports causes that champion the empowerment of women and their families. She serves as a mentor and advocate for women in her local community. As a spirited sponsor for the war to end domestic violence, she works to bring awareness and funding to organizations supporting this mission.

Mary received her Ph.D. in Administration and Management from Walden University. Her doctoral dissertation, titled *HMOs, NCQA, and Public Interest Regulation,* was published nationally. Currently pursuing her law degree part-time at the Phoenix School of Law, upon graduation Mary plans to donate her legal services to domestic violence victims in her local community.

Mary and her husband, Eric, live in Phoenix, AZ.

Contact
Dr. Mary Fischer-McKee
mfmckee@cox.net

THREE

WHAT IS A LEADER?

By Mary Fischer-McKee, Ph.D.

What is a Leader?

This has been a question for the ages. Literally, thousands of books have been written on the subject with varying quality. As I begun my journey on the road to leadership, I struggled to find reference materials that addressed the insecurity I felt as a new leader. The origins of this chapter can be traced to my introduction to leadership – my call to leadership and my early struggles as a leader. As I write this chapter today, I benefit from several years of direct leadership experience, as well as the shared experiences I have gained by serving as a leadership mentor to others. These experiences have been combined with my own field research and collectively serve as the real-world foundation of the (BRAVE)^2 leadership profile.

The Call To Be A Leader

Through the years I have been privileged to serve as a mentor to many women. These women were on all points of the career spectrum – women just starting out in the workforce, women looking to move up within an organization, and women who were looking to branch out on their own. Each of these women represented a unique combination of life experience, career experience, and career ambition. And while each of them represented their own unique hopes and dreams, they also shared a strong common desire – the desire to make a difference in the lives of their families, their workplaces, and their communities. And for some of these women, that desire created a spark – a spark that ignited into a call to be a leader.

The call to be a leader shows up in different ways for different women. There are women who were born with a call to lead. Other women are called to become leaders by circumstance, and still others are called to become leaders as the result of a life-changing experience. This is how I was called to be a leader. For many years, I, like many of you, found myself afraid to fully live my life. I knew what I wanted to do, but I was often too afraid or too intimidated to take the necessary steps to do it. You see, I was an observer of life. (Not to sell myself short, by most accounts I was a gifted observer.) I partnered with the right people, educated myself, and rapidly moved up the corporate ladder. Everything looked great from the outside, but deep down inside I was stuck.

Having been part of a family start-up business in my early twenties, I learned a lot about business and people. And although I had achieved a respectable measure of professional success at a young age, I was holding myself back. I could observe situations and assimilate information like nobody's business, but what I hadn't learned to do was trust myself and to trust my decisions. I had lots of ideas of what I wanted to do, but instead of taking action, I spent my time preoccupied with the fear that I would make a mistake. So instead of stepping up, I waited in the background for someone else to take the lead. And guess what! Someone else always did. On the surface this was an ingenious construct; when I left the family business I was able to build a very lucrative career serving as the brains and support behind strong business leaders. Then in the early 1990s, something changed for me.

It started as a small but insistent discontent with my role in the business world; a nagging doubt that I wasn't doing what I was meant to do. At first, I wasn't quite sure what was going on. I worked for and with good people. I had an important and challenging job. Yet, I was very unhappy. And then the realization came to me – my behind-the-scenes role wasn't enough for me anymore; I was being to called to do more – to be more. This realization came to me in a personal growth seminar, and at that seminar I began to take the next step in my personal and professional development. The result of which became the foundation for my path to becoming a leader.

During an exercise in the seminar, I was called upon to make a difficult decision that would not only impact my ability to continue in the seminar, but also impacted the participation of several others. Front and center I stood – no leader to look to for guidance, no one else to make a tough call, and no powerful person to hide behind – no excuses. I knew the right thing to do. I knew what I wanted to do, but when I looked around the room – at the faces staring at me – that old uncertainty crippled me. Thoughts raced through my mind – holding me back – telling me that no one else was sticking their neck out – why should I? The "what ifs" filled my mind. "What if I broke the rules?" "What if I got kicked out of the seminar?" "What if I was wrong and made a mistake in front of everyone?" It was during that seminar that I first heard the words that would become the mantra for my personal and professional growth. The facilitator stood next to me speaking in a quiet voice, and said, "Mary, what if it were up to you?" It was a call for me to do the right thing. It was a call for me to face my fears, even when no one else was willing to do it. It was a call for me to become a leader. It felt like an eternity to break through – to answer the call to be the leader that I was meant to be. In actuality, it took about thirty-five minutes, but the power of that thirty-five minutes changed the course of both my personal and professional life.

What I learned in that seminar introduced me to the exhilaration of being a leader – being the one willing to step up, take a risk, and make a difference. Unfortunately, with as powerful as that experience was, it didn't do much to prepare me for what it meant to be a leader on a daily basis. The spark was ignited, and I had answered the call, but very quickly I was left asking myself, "Okay, now what?"

A job change shortly after the seminar provided me with my first professional opportunity to be a leader. That change helped me to start spreading my wings, and gave me the opportunity to experiment with different leadership concepts. And while some of my experiments were more successful than others, the experimentation did very little for my confidence as a leader. In those early years, I jumped from one trendy leadership technique to another, often changing my mind in the middle. I often felt like a fraud, pretending to know what to do and why I was doing it, when the truth was, I literally had no idea what I was doing, and the folks on my team knew it.

I struggled to find a female mentor who would admit to ever having the insecurity I was feeling. As it turns out, at least at that time, there were very few women leaders out there willing to admit that they didn't have it all together. And let's face it – women have fought long and hard to make it to the leadership ranks. The last thing they wanted to admit to anyone was that they had struggled with their confidence. I went everywhere to find help. I went to the library, to seminars, and to networking groups. As a life-long student, I was certain I would find a book to provide me with real-world, practical advice. There have been literally thousands of books written on leadership, yet I struggled to find a book that addressed my questions. Then one day I found myself in the bookstore (again) looking through the business section, and I found myself asking why it was so difficult to find that I was looking for. My mind flashed back to that life-changing moment in the seminar and the magic question popped into my head – "Mary, what if it were up to you?" Once again that simple question served as my call to action.

The (BRAVE)² Leadership Profile

In addition to my own experimentation, I did some field research. I talked with a lot of other people (leaders and non-leaders) to get their thoughts on what it took to be an effective leader. My research confirmed my worst fear. People want certainty – they want courageous and confident leaders. And wouldn't you know it, confidence was one of the things that I struggled with most as a new leader. For me, there was a big difference between being called to be a leader and being able to pull it off with confidence. Those early years were a constant struggle.

Early in my research to develop a "real-world" reference guide for new leaders, I came across a quote by Corra May White Harris that struck a chord with me. She said, "The bravest thing you can do when you are not brave is to profess courage and act accordingly." I quickly went to the dictionary to look up the word *brave*. The New Lexicon Webster's Encyclopedic Dictionary defines brave as "bold, courageous, mastering fear." Boldness, courage, and the ability to master fear are all things that an individual needs as they take on the challenge of leading others. And such became the inspiration for the (BRAVE)^2 leadership profile.

The (BRAVE)^2 leadership profile is comprised of ten easy-to-remember leadership behaviors and supporting narrative designed to support you to confidently develop the skills necessary to become an effective leader.

	(1)	(2)
B	**Begins**	**Believes**
R	**Risk-taker**	**Rewards**
A	**Able**	**Aware**
V	**Visible**	**Vigilant**
E	**Enrolls**	**Empowers**

B(1) – Begins

"All glory comes from daring to begin." —Eugene F. Ware

The difference between a (BRAVE)^2 leader and everyone else is that a (BRAVE)^2 leader actually begins to take action while others let fear hold them back. She knows that for many people it is easier to sit on the sidelines than to jump into the game. Her eagerness to tackle the challenge in front of her liberates others to join in and support her cause.

B(2) – Believes

"In order to succeed, we must first believe that we can." —Michael Korda

The difference between a (BRAVE)^2 leader and everyone else is that a (BRAVE)^2 leader is a true believer. She believes in her cause, her vision, and most importantly her team. She is passionate about her beliefs and inspires those around her to feel that passion as well.

R(1) – Risk-Taker

"Even if you are on the right track,
you will get run over if you just sit there." —Will Rogers

The difference between a (BRAVE)^2 leader and everyone else is that a (BRAVE)^2 leader is willing to take risks. She is not one to throw caution to the wind, but she is willing to take calculated risks to support the development of her ideas, her team, and the future of her cause.

R(2) – Rewards

"In the arena of human life the honors and rewards fall to those who show their good qualities in action." —Aristotle

The difference between a (BRAVE)^2 leader and everyone else is that a (BRAVE)^2 leader rewards her team for the right behaviors. She is emotionally invested in her team members and their development. She not only rewards her team members for a job well done, but she also rewards them with recognition and support as they take risks to learn and grow.

A(1) – Able

"When I've heard all I need to make a decision, I don't take a vote. I make a decision." —Ronald Reagan

The difference between a (BRAVE)^2 leader and everyone else is that a (BRAVE)^2 leader is able and willing to make the tough calls. She knows that 90% of leadership is making decisions. She also knows that the success of her team is dependent upon her ability to make the tough decisions when required.

A(2) – Aware

"To handle yourself, use your head; to handle others, use your heart." —Donald Laird

The difference between a (BRAVE)^2 leader and everyone else is that a (BRAVE)^2 leader is aware of the impact her decisions have on others. She understands that a team is made up of individuals, and that her decisions can impact their lives, both positively and negatively. She is aware that an effective leader must balance both her heart and her head when making decisions.

V(1) – Visible

"If you wait for people to come to you, you'll only get small problems. You must go and find them. The big problems are where people don't realize they have one in the first place." —W. Edwards Deming

The difference between a (BRAVE)^2 leader and everyone else is that a (BRAVE)^2 leader is visible and accessible to her team. She knows that the most important things happen in between formal meetings. She knows that to truly understand what is going on, she can't lead from an ivory tower; she needs to be available to her team for big things and small.

V(2) – Vigilant

"Setting an example is not the main means of influencing others; it is the only means." Albert Einstein

The difference between a (BRAVE)^2 leader and everyone else is that a (BRAVE)^2 leader is always vigilant. She knows that she is always on stage and that her team watches her energy and actions and then mimics them. She knows if her actions and words are inconsistent, her team and results will also be inconsistent.

E(1) – Enrolls

"A mediocre idea that generates enthusiasm will go further than a great idea that inspires no one." —Mary Kay Ash

The difference between a (BRAVE)^2 leader and everyone else is that a (BRAVE)^2 leader does not command by rank or intimidation; she enrolls people into her vision. She shares her vision and her passion for it in equal measures. She knows that to enroll people, she must inspire and motivate them.

E(2) - Empowers

> *"If you tell people where to go, but not how to get there, you'll be amazed at the results."* —General George S. Patton

The difference between a (BRAVE)^2 leader and everyone else is that a (BRAVE)^2 leader knows that she must empower the people around her. She knows that she cannot do everything on her own. She surrounds herself with a competent team, provides them with the necessary tools and support, and trusts them to get the job done.

Using (BRAVE) ^{2}

This chapter and the (BRAVE)^2 leadership profile was developed to support you on three distinct levels. The first level is to assure you that you are not alone. It is my sincere hope that my story serves as an inspiration to you as you develop your confidence as a leader. The second level is to serve as a road map to developing the essential behaviors of a (BRAVE)^2 leader. I recommend that you focus on developing one of the ten leadership behaviors each week. Your confidence will build as you begin to master a behavior. The third level is to serve as reinforcement to your (BRAVE)^2 program. Once you complete your (BRAVE)^2 program, I invite you to go back and work on the behaviors that gave you the most trouble. Photocopy the (BRAVE)^2 behavior narrative and quotation. Glue it to an index card and place it somewhere where you can see it on a regular basis. Challenge yourself to find opportunities to use this behavior in your everyday life. Your hard work will pay off, I promise.

"Leaders aren't born, they are made. And they are made just like anything else, through hard work. And that's the price we'll have to pay to achieve that goal, or any goal." —Vincent Lombardi

The bottom line is this – it doesn't matter how you were called to be a leader, it doesn't matter how much or how little education you have, and it doesn't matter how long you have been working - everyone is afraid when they first become a leader. Don't give up! By working hard and incorporating the (BRAVE)^2 leadership behaviors into your daily routine, you are already on the road to becoming to positive, passionate and productive leader.

What is a leader? A leader is (BRAVE)^2.

ABOUT THE AUTHOR

BRENDA MCDOWELL-HOLMES, MBA

Brenda McDowell-Holmes is Founder, President and Chief Executive Officer of McDowell-Holmes & Associates, Inc. The company was established in 2005 to provide personal and professional development services for youth, school districts, business professionals and organizations of all sizes.

McDowell-Holmes & Associates has successfully mentored and counseled youth to overcome obstacles to fulfilling their life purpose. Youth development sessions include Save Our Youth, Stress Management for Youth and Leadership Development. The company also conducts personal and professional development seminars on various topics, including marketing strategies for consultants, women's issues, diversity, wellness and branding and image projection.

Ms. McDowell-Holmes is a veteran of diversified experience in the corporate environment. She is certified in Diversity, Professional Speaking, Customer Service and Youth Issues. She holds a Masters Degree in Business Administration/Human Resources and a Bachelors Degree in Business Administration/Management. Ms. McDowell-Holmes is also a member of several professional organizations, such as Professional Woman Network (Advisory Board), American Business Women's Association, National Association for Female Executives and National Black MBA Association and Toastmasters International. She is also a Real Estate investor.

Ms. McDowell-Holmes is the co-author of several soon to be released books: *A Women's Guide for Overcoming Obstacles, Transition & Change, Women s Leaders: Strategies for Empowerment & Communication, and Beyond the Body: Developing Inner Beauty.*

She dedicates this book project to her wonderful father and her beautiful mother and angel. I truly believe in angels. My father Mr. Abraham McDowell is still committed to watching over their children, even after his wife's death. Thank you daddy for believing in me and now I can help ***motivate people to change their lives***.

Ms. McDowell-Holmes is available to conduct seminars and workshops on a local, national and international basis.

Contact
McDowell-Holmes & Associates, Inc.
P.O. Box 1583
Stockbridge, Ga. 30281
(404) 663-2418
brholmes@bellsouth.net
www.protrain.net

FOUR

TRANSITIONING TO A NEW CAREER

By Brenda J. McDowell-Holmes

Do You Want a New Career?

When you think about your career, do you get excited because you are living your dream, or do you feel trapped in a job you don't like simply because it provides you with a feeling of security? If you happen to be in the group who doesn't enjoy their work, you should ask yourself if you are stopping yourself from transitioning to a new career because of your fears. Are you afraid you won't make enough money in your new career to support yourself and your family? Are you anxious about a potential loss in benefits that your current job provides? While these are very real concerns, you also need to realize what's at stake: your happiness. Do you want to come to the end of your life only to realize that your work wasn't fulfilling, and that you spent most of your time doing something you didn't enjoy?

One thing you can do is to evaluate where you are in your career right now, and whether you find your work to be fulfilling.

Exercise #1

On the line to the left of the statement, write a number from 1-5. Score "1" if you strongly disagree, "2" if you disagree, "3" if you are neutral, "4" if you agree, and "5" if you strongly agree.

_____ 1. I enjoy my job.

_____ 2. I look forward to going to work every day.

_____ 3. My job challenges me.

_____ 4. I am able to utilize my knowledge and skills in my work.

_____ 5. I am encouraged to use my creative abilities on my job.

_____ 6. I would do my job even if I didn't get paid for it.

_____ 7. I would continue doing my job even if it didn't include any benefits.

_____ 8. I find my job rewarding and fulfilling.

_____ 9. I can't believe how fast the time passes when I am on the job.

_____ 10. I am happy when I am at work.

*If you scored **20 or less**, you need to start looking for another job immediately, possibly in a completely different line of work. If you scored from **21-39**, you need to seriously consider making some changes either in your current job situation or in your present career path. If you scored **40 or more**, you are going in the right direction with your career.*

Even if you love your current job, you need to be aware that changes in the economy can result in layoffs. In fact, most people in this day and age no longer work at the same company all their lives. As a result, career transitions are quite common, so it is a good idea to be prepared for a different job, or even a completely new line of work. But where do you start, and how can you move through your career transition successfully? One of the most important things you can do is to plan to succeed. A well-organized plan is vital to a successful career transition. So you should have a plan to achieve your goals.

Tips for Planning A New Career.

If you are seriously thinking about a career transition, take a few moments to think about these tips to help you plan to be successful:

- **Set Aside Some Time for Your Job Search.** Changing jobs or careers requires work and lots of research, which may take a tremendous amount of time. So be aware that you will need to schedule some time for this process.

- **Get Real and be Honest.** Your goal is to make a successful career change with realistic goals based on an honest assessment of your skills. Obviously you can't suddenly become a pro athlete or brain surgeon if you haven't had any training for these jobs.

- **Search the Firms and Not the Want Ads.** You will have better results looking for the companies that you are interested in working for. Look up the 100 top companies to work for". (This can be researched by Internet.) You should even consider firms who are paid to find highly experienced talent to match the job openings for a particular employer.

- **Find a True Mentor.** This will be a person who provides guidance, facilitates introductions, and endorses your capabilities. A true mentor is a person who really cares, and is not just helping because he/she is told to do so by the company.

- **Volunteer.** Find a place where you can be an intern. This will help you learn about the business while you gain experience. The more experience you have in your chosen career path, the more you can increase your skill set, and the more desirable you will be to potential employers.

- **Learn the Language.** Every company or industry has its own language and values associated with its corporate culture. Get acquainted with your particular industry and its needs. Learning everything you can will improve your knowledge and skills. For example, I worked in the transportation industry for many years; however, while doing so, I learned about other companies and what they did to achieve success.

- **Learn the Business.** Read, read, read about the industry that you are interested in. Check the Internet and the library in order to get some background information about the company's policies and the current issues they are facing. Company decision makers are impressed when a potential employee takes the time to become more familiar with their industry.

- **Keep Your Resume Up-to-Date.** You want to be prepared if a potential employer asks to see your credentials. As a result, you should always keep a current copy of your resume handy, even if you are not actively searching for a job at the present time. Make sure all your contact information is up-to-date and that your latest employment history is listed.

- **Network, Network, Network.** Yes, you have heard this before, but networking is one of the most important things you can do as you search for a new career. Networking as a tool for career development seems to be gaining in popularity, especially among women. During the past few years, people have come to recognize the importance of connecting with others. When people get together with a common goal, task, or social need in mind, informal networks are often formed. More formal networks form when a specified group agrees to meet regularly, as a way to provide a mutual benefit among members through the sharing of information.

Choosing A Career Path.

While some people know what they want to do from a very early age, others struggle to find the exact job that will make them happy. If you are one of the people who is having a hard time deciding exactly what you want to do for your career, try the following exercise.

Exercise #2

In the left column below, write down the things you are good at that you also enjoy doing. These things can include things like playing with children, watching television, playing video games, etc. In the right column, write down the types of jobs that might incorporate your skills/talents/interests. So, if you like playing with children, you might consider a job at a daycare. If you enjoy watching T.V., a job watching surveillance video cameras might work for you. If you want to spend hours playing video games, you might consider a career in video game development or design. Don't limit yourself to jobs you feel you are qualified to do at the present time. Remember, you can always go back and get the training you need in order to be able to pursue your dream career.

SKILLS/TALENTS/INTERESTS	POSSIBLE JOBS

After looking at the above list, prioritize the things you are most interested in by numbering them with #1, #2, #3, etc. with #1 being your top choice. Now, do some research on what kind of training you would need to pursue this career path. If you have to go back to school, how much will it cost you and how long will it take? Can you commit to that kind of investment? Is it worth it to you? What can you do in the meantime? Could you pursue one of the other careers on your list that wouldn't require any additional training while you are preparing yourself for your dream job? An honest assessment of your commitment level is required here. You need to know what you are willing to sacrifice in order to pursue a career that will make you happy. Really consider what job(s) you are passionate about doing. If you are passionate about a certain job or career, then you should be willing to make some sacrifices in order to attain it. This might even include a cut in pay or a decrease in benefits. You need to really think hard about what is most important to you in life. Are you more concerned about making money or being happy? Is there a way you can have both by making some sacrifices now that will pay off in bigger dividends later in your career?

Tips for Transitioning Into A New Career.

Taking the steps necessary to pursue a new career path is not always easy. However, here are a few tips to help you transition into a new career and feel more confident about you.

1. **Have a Desire to Change.** Have you ever felt so down that you realized you had to make a change in what you were doing because there had to be something better for you in life? This would be a sign that you are not going to be complete unless you take action to satisfy your desire. Do not be afraid to move forward in life. You never know what you can do until you try. Stop making excuses for why you don't want to make a change. If you really have the desire to change your career, take the very first step you need to take in order to make it happen.

2. **Take Immediate Action.** What are you going to do about the changes that you want in your life? The steps you decide to take toward attaining your new career goal will determine your commitment to making this change. Take immediate action by updating your resume, researching companies in your field, taking a class on the subject, etc. Stop waiting for your present company to promote you. Determine what you desire to do and how long you are willing to work towards your goals. It all starts with your thoughts. Think outside of the box beyond what you are now doing and envision yourself doing something you love.

3. **Make a Career Shift**. Once you have made up your mind to change your career/job, then never look back. Stick to your plan and plan to succeed – no matter how difficult it may seem. Sometimes we are creatures of habit and get in a comfort zone, doing the same thing over and over because we are afraid to change. However, it is important to accept the challenge of doing something new and different in life. All you have to do is simply apply the skills you already have to a new industry and/or a better company. Just start looking for a position which offers incentives that are important to you: a better work environment, more recognition, better pay, less commuting time, a more favorable chance for advancement, etc. Focus on those things that will make you happy and improve both your self-esteem and quality of life. After all, you deserve the best life has to offer.

4. **Recognize Your Skills.** First, you should list all the things you are good at doing. This will help you recognize your worth and what you have to offer any company that hires you. Second, you should develop a personal profile of your skills, listing things like your best work environment and what type of job would really make you happy. The happier you are, the more productive you will be. For example, I really enjoy working with people instead of working alone. What type of person are you? Would your rather work on a computer by yourself in a cubicle or greet customers when they walk in the front door? By recognizing your personal preferences, you will be better able to identify the kinds of jobs that you will enjoy. Third, you should sell yourself to a new employer by showing them how you can be an asset to their company. Discuss how you benefited the companies you worked for in the past, using

numbers and percentages whenever possible. For example, you could say that you increased productivity by 12% and decreased waste by 8%. Be specific about the exact things you will do for your new employer so they can see you are serious about your work and how you can help their company.

5. **Do Some Self-Evaluation.** Take some "me time" to really think about what you want from your work and your career. Can you envision yourself having the job that you really want? Use your senses to imagine what that job will look like, sound like, feel like, etc. Change how you see yourself. For instance, if you want to be a manager, start viewing yourself that way. Do the things a manager does. Act the way a manager acts. Then before you know it, you will be the manager you want to be. Think about the amount of preparation you have undergone for your prospective career. Have you taken enough classes in your field? Do you have the type of trade experience required for the position you are seeking? If not, consider doing some volunteer work. You will benefit greatly because of the experience. Volunteering can give you a sneak peek into the job you think you want so you can see if it is really for you. It can also offer you the chance to take on different leadership roles. The most important thing about volunteering is to be true to yourself and learn from your experience.

6. **Set Goals.** Plan to succeed by writing down your goals. Having something down on paper will allow you to revisit your thoughts. After writing down what you want to achieve, set a certain time frame to follow. How many years or months do you need to accomplish what you want to do? Break these down into things you can achieve each week and then further break them down into

what you must do each day. By taking daily action toward your dreams, you can make them a concrete reality. Believe that you can achieve your goals. Stay positive, even if you run into some rough times while on the path toward seeking a better job. Sometimes the obstacles you encounter may make it appear as if you will not be able to achieve your goals. But remember that your dream will happen if you just continue to keep working toward your goals. You may have to modify the plan at times and put more effort into things like networking, but you should never give up. Anything worth having requires a great deal of work. So just stick to your daily schedule and before you know it, your dream job will be the one you are waking up to do each day.

7. **Research and Explore Your Options While Maintaining Balance.** Go online, read books, take classes, and network with other people in order to get the vital information you need about your prospective industry. But also take some time to enjoy life while you are researching the job market. It is very important to have some balance in your life. If you are spending all your time looking for a new job, then you are neglecting other important areas of your life, like your family, health, and spiritual growth. It's important to live a little and laugh a little while balancing your job search with the other essential things in your life.

8. **Think Like a Recruiter.** What kinds of skills would a recruiter want from a potential employee in your field of interest? By putting yourself in the position of the recruiter, you will be able to think of the questions you may be asked during an interview, and will be better able to prepare yourself to make a good impression when you are being evaluated as a potential candidate for your dream job.

A Successful Career Transition

A successful career transition is possible for anyone willing to do the work necessary to make it happen. Although leaving your comfort zone can sometimes be scary, it is essential to your growth as an individual. If you are not continually striving to reach your dreams, you are stagnating and dragging yourself down with excuses for why you can't have everything you want in life. A successful career transition depends on you. It depends on your willingness to change and to risk learning something new. It depends on your ability to see yourself as the person you want to be with the job you want to have. It depends on how much you want to be happy, and how much you are willing to sacrifice to achieve your dreams. Do you believe that you can achieve? Are you a dreamer? Don't stop dreaming, because dreams are where visions of a new reality are created. If you want to succeed, start today making your career dreams a reality.

ABOUT THE AUTHOR

HAZEL BLAKE-PARKER

Hazel Blake Parker is Chief Executive Officer of The Parker Institute for Excellence, LLP and Director of Staff Development and Training for the South Carolina Department of Social Services. She has gained extensive knowledge and experience in management, training and family life issues through these positions. She has developed, coordinated, facilitated and evaluated training sessions for groups that have included all levels of staff from administrative assistants to executive staff.

Ms. Parker established The Parker Institute for Excellence, LLP in 2001 to provide personal and professional development training seminars to all types of organizations. Topics include Diversity, Conflict Resolution, Customer Service, Parenting, Effective Supervision, Leadership, and Communication. She also conducts grant writing workshops, writes and reviews proposals for nonprofit organizations and assists organizations in obtaining nonprofit status. She has been a certified grant writer since 1998.

As Training Director, Ms. Parker develops and monitors over $8 million in training contracts and manages a division responsible for training over 4,000 DSS employees statewide. Training sessions encompass policies and procedures, as well as skills development, leadership, facilitation skills and e-learning. Ms. Parker has worked for the agency for over 23 years in various capacities, from frontline caseworker to manager.

Ms. Parker is involved in many organizations, including Edisto Fork United Methodist Church, American Society for Training and Development, Child Evangelism Fellowship, National Association for Female Executives and National Council on Family Relations. She is also a member of the International Board of Advisors for the Professional Woman Network. She resides in Orangeburg, South Carolina with her husband, Terry, and son, Taurean.

Contact:
The Parker Institute for Excellence, LLP
P.O. Box 2438
Orangeburg, SC 29116
(803) 347-5627
parkerinstitute@oburg.net
www.parkerinstitute.com
www.protrain.net

FIVE

20 TIPS FOR DYNAMIC PRESENTATIONS AND MEETINGS

By Hazel Blake-Parker

Meetings and presentations are a way of life in many organizations, and are often a primary means of communicating information among staff. Even with the increased use of various types of technology such as e-mail, webcasting and teleconferences, meetings and presentations are still common and necessary. With tight schedules, telecommuting, flexible work hours and multiple office locations, organizations must maximize the effectiveness of meetings and presentations so that employees do not feel that their time is being wasted. While meetings and presentations are quite distinct activities, the planning processes for both are relatively similar. This chapter will highlight tips and techniques that will make your meetings and presentations productive and meaningful.

Communicate. Since the primary purpose of any meeting or presentation is to impart information, the most critical skill you need to develop is effective communication. This entails a myriad of skills such as speech clarity, volume, pitch, rate of speech, facial expressions, eye contact and body language. Mastering these skills will ensure that your intended message is delivered. These three communication tips are vital in effectively delivering your presentation:

- Enunciation

    o   Use correct grammar. This increases your credibility.

    o   Pronounce words clearly and correctly.

    o   Avoid audibles, such as uh, um and ah, when speaking. While a few may not be very noticeable, overuse gives the appearance of being unprepared.

- Voice

    o   Speak deliberately, at an average pace. Avoid sounding rushed.

    o   Speak so that you are clearly audible. Use a microphone, if necessary.

    o   Vary voice pitch for emphasis and to avoid speaking in a monotonous tone.

    o   Control your tone to avoid sounding harsh.

- Nonverbals

    o   Use facial expressions appropriately. Look pleasant and genuine. Participants perceive you as friendly, warm and approachable when your expressions are positive.

    o   Maintain frequent eye contact. Avoid staring, "talking to the screen" or turning your back to participants for extended periods of time. Eye contact conveys interest and increases your credibility.

    o   Move around naturally; avoid pacing or rocking.

    o   Maintain an open, relaxed stance. Avoid standing rigidly or slouching.

    o   Use open gestures, such as open hands, leaning forward and head nods to show your willingness to communicate. Avoid annoying gestures, such as jingling coins in pockets, fidgeting, and playing with clothing or jewelry. Use appropriate gestures to add animation to the presentation.

Prepare. Great meetings and presentations do not just happen. You must first plan and prepare. The old saying "If you fail to plan, plan to fail" is never truer than when it comes to meetings and presentations. Lack of adequate preparation will be very apparent, even for experienced speakers. Follow these five tips to assure that you are amply prepared for your next meeting or presentation:

- *Plan your agenda and set objectives* to be accomplished so that discussions and activities are structured to meet desired outcomes.

When planning for a meeting, involve the participants in developing the agenda so that they come better prepared for discussion, and the meeting can be more focused. Similarly, training objectives guide the presentation and communicates what will be learned in the session. It provides a road map of sorts that leads to the desired learning outcome.

- *Proofread all materials.* Documents that contain typographical or grammatical errors reduce your credibility. Make copies of handouts in advance and have enough for the entire group.

- *Know your stuff.* Learn as much as you can about the topic on which you're speaking. Research the topic thoroughly, and if possible, interview an expert or get some experience in the area. You will likely be unable to answer questions or give concrete examples to facilitate participants' understanding without a thorough knowledge of the topic. Lack of preparation may cause participants to resent their time being wasted.

- *Check audio/visual equipment.* If your presentation requires equipment, check it in advance for operability and to be sure you know how to use it. It is advisable to practice using the equipment in advance to enhance your confidence during your presentation.

- *Examine the room in advance.* This allows you to plan in advance how you will set it up to accommodate your group and any props or equipment you need.

Define Your Audience. Another important aspect of having dynamic meetings and presentations is defining your audience. For meetings, having the appropriate people in attendance is key. If the right people are not present, important decisions cannot be made and the absentees must be briefed after the meeting. For presentations, you must know who your participants are and what their needs are. This will allow you to customize your content to meet their needs and expectations, as well as help you meet your objectives. To define your audience, ask the following questions:

- What are their professions, titles or responsibilities?

- What is their reason for attending your training?

- What is their area of expertise?

- What information do they need to do their jobs effectively?

- How much do they already know about your topic?

Customizing your presentation to fit the audience creates a more positive environment during the session and produces better learning outcomes for participants.

Consider Learning Styles. Another consideration for effective meetings and presentations is the learning styles of participants. Most people tend to be predominantly one type of learner – visual, auditory or kinesthetic. Therefore, in order to present effectively, you must cater to all learning styles. It is beneficial to know your dominant learning style because you will tend to present from this perspective. Before we discuss how to appeal to learners, take the following brief inventory to determine your learning style.

Table 1

Determining Your Learning Style

Circle the number in the chart below that corresponds to each statement that is true about you. The column with the most items circled represents your primary learning style.

1. I'd rather listen to a lecture than do assigned reading.

2. I prefer to read on my own to learn something.

3. I need to do the task myself in order to learn how to do it.

4. I can learn by simply watching a demonstration.

5. I like to use computers.

6. My understanding is improved by seeing illustrations and diagrams.

7. I prefer courses that involve physical activity.

8. I like to listen to audiotapes of lessons.

9. I like labs better than lectures because of the hands-on experience.

10. Class discussions are helpful to me.

11. Manuals and printed directions are helpful to me.

12. I follow directions best when they are read to me.

VISUAL	AUDITORY	KINESTHETIC
2	1	3
4	8	5

6	10	7
11	12	9

My primary learning style is: _____.

Now that you know your learning style, use the following chart to design your presentation so that it will appeal to all attendees.

Table 2
Effective Techniques For Each Learning Style

VISUAL	AUDITORY	KINESTHETIC
Demonstrations	Group discussions	Physical examples
Copying notes	Lectures	Experiments
Highlighting key points in manuals/books/notes	Music	Role playing
Videos	Repeating ideas orally	Problem solving
Guided imagery	Audiotapes	Games/Exercises

Give It a Name. In order to have an audience, there must be something to attract them. Thus, the title or topic is important. Would you read an article if the headline did not sound interesting? Probably not. The same goes for your meeting or presentation. If the topic does not arouse people's curiosity, they will not attend. Think of your topic as the headline for your local paper and name it accordingly. Would you rather attend "Communicating Effectively" or "How to Be Me & Still Like You"?

Capture Audience Attention. Begin your session by capturing the audience's attention. Even if they are not attending voluntarily, a dynamic opening may turn them into a willing participant. There are several ways to get started effectively:

- State a startling statistic or unusual fact that relates to your topic.

- Make a controversial statement.

- Ask a rhetorical question.

- Involve the audience. Conducting a brief icebreaker is an excellent technique.

- Make them laugh. Appropriate humor can release tension and get the audience enthusiastic about the rest of the presentation.

A memorable opener can make the difference between a memorable event and a forgettable one.

Engage Your Audience. Once you have their attention, you must keep your audience engaged throughout the presentation. Variety is the key to accomplishing this task. The average adult attention span is about 20 minutes; therefore, you need to vary your delivery method at least every 15-20 minutes to avoid boredom and mental vacations. Common ways of presenting information in different ways include:

- Presenting a case study. Participants can work in groups to devise a solution.

- Using role playing to have participants practice a new skill or behavior

- Telling a story

- Lecturing

- Asking questions to generate group discussion

- Playing video or audio clips

In addition to reducing boredom and keeping the presentation interesting, using various training methods stimulates everyone to participate, appeals to most learning styles, and increases participant knowledge.

Add a Multimedia Component. Audio and visual clips and PowerPoint presentations can add pizzazz to even the most mundane information. They add variety, reinforce learning points, and make presentations more persuasive. When using video and audio clips, limit them to 5 to 10 minutes, maximum. For longer clips, stop them periodically for discussion. Videos are an excellent means of bringing the "expert" into the training, and for providing real-life examples.

PowerPoint presentations have become a very popular tool in meetings and presentations. Keep the following tips in mind when using slide presentations:

- They are training guides only. Do not put your entire presentation on the slides.

- Use short bulleted points rather than sentences.

- Use a serif (footed) font. It will be easier for participants to read.

- Use pictures, but do not crowd the slide.

- Be familiar with the information so that you do not have to read each slide.

While multimedia can be wonderful supplements to your meeting or presentation, they can also be a source of frustration to both the presenter and participants if technical problems arise. Ensure that you are familiar with how to use all equipment and have spare bulbs, etc. that may be needed. It is a good idea to have either a flipchart or whiteboard available to record information from the group, or to use as a "parking lot" for issues to be discussed later or at a subsequent meeting.

Develop Handouts. Creating eye-catching handouts or training manuals can create interest in your topic and be used as tools to help participants learn. Whether you have just a few pages or a workbook/manual, developing effective handouts can help your audience to continue learning long after the presentation is over. To develop effective handouts:

- *Customize handouts* so that they focus on what you are trying to accomplish. Each one should be relevant and highlight key learning points.

- *Create worksheet style handouts.* Handouts are a visual aid that supplements your presentation – it is NOT the entire presentation. Include white space for note-taking and leave several bulleted points blank so that participants can fill them in. People only remember 10% of what is heard after a few days. Having participants fill in information facilitates learning and aids retention.

- *Make handouts appealing.* Use various page layouts, pictures, and clip art to make handouts appealing. Great training materials increase participant interest in the presentation, as well as confidence in the trainer.

Respect Audience's Time. How many times have you gone to a meeting or training session that started late? What did you think of the presenter? Your credibility is on the line if you start late or run over the allotted time. First, commit to starting on time and try to finish a few minutes early. Then continue with the agenda as latecomers arrive, without stopping to "catch them up." This is punitive to the prompt arrivers. You can even have a little fun with latecomers by having a "zinger jar," whereby they will be required to deposit a quarter (or other amount) for each minute they are late. At the end of the session, you could hold a raffle or, if it was a meeting within your office, buy treats for the next meeting. The list below contains additional information concerning meeting time management.

- Starting on time sends the message that you are serious about your topic, and that you value your audience's time.

- Be concise and stay focused on the agenda/objectives. This will decrease the likelihood of going beyond the allotted time.

- Design the agenda to allow time for discussion and questions. If issues arise that cannot be resolved, table them (put on the parking lot) for a future meeting, or research them and follow up with participants.

- Appoint a timekeeper to keep momentum flowing. This person can monitor activities, discussions, breaks, etc. and notify the presenter when it is time to move on.

- If time starts to run out, solicit input from the group as to how to handle the information still to be presented.

When time is well managed, participants feel that they have had a good experience, and that their time was well spent.

Establish Rapport. The ability to establish and maintain rapport with your audience is an important soft skill that can make or break your session. How would you feel if you walked into a room and the presenter immediately began training? Do you think you would want to stay? Whether you are familiar with the audience or not, you need to establish a comfortable and inviting learning atmosphere. Simple gestures such as greeting participants at the door, small talk during breaks, eye contact, and sharing information about yourself go a long way toward displaying that you are approachable. Conducting a brief icebreaker with the group is also an excellent way to get the group to know one another. Establishing rapport creates a climate of trust, creativity and open sharing – all critical to the learning process.

Tame the Session Dragons. There are often participants who hold sidebar conversations, antagonize the presenter with needless questions, or otherwise cause problems in the session. When this happens, your first goal is to stop the behavior immediately to maintain control of the group and the integrity of the meeting or presentation. Repeat interruptions of this kind annoy other participants, and possibly make them uncomfortable. You have several options to handle difficult participants:

- Keep them engaged to lessen their opportunity to misbehave.

- Ignore the behavior if it is minor. If it recurs, handle it.

- Set limits on questions and discussions. Ask that those with additional questions speak with you after class.

- For sidebar conversations, move toward the individuals and speak from that spot for a few minutes. The attention of the entire group focused in their direction stops the conversation.

- Directly address the issue. If you must resort to this technique, be respectful of the participant. Do not embarrass or belittle him/her.

Conquer Your Imaginary Dragons. Fear of public speaking is often the cause of great anxiety. "Being on stage" takes confidence and competence. While you do need to be prepared, you do not need to be perfect. You will occasionally make mistakes, trip over a cord, or forget to do something. So how do you conquer this fear? First of all, relax and take a deep breath. Then concentrate on your delivery. Think about the communication tips mentioned earlier – control your speed and volume and pay attention to your nonverbals. Treat mistakes as opportunities to improve, and identify your fears upfront. A little fear provides you with extra energy to get you through the presentation. More importantly, be yourself, believe in what you are saying, and do not hesitate to laugh at yourself. Your audience will appreciate this display of genuineness.

Close the Deal. A fantastic finish is just as important as a great start. The closing part of any meeting or presentation should tie the entire session together. For meetings, the closing should summarize points covered, decisions made, assignments given, and timeframes for completion of assigned tasks. Closing the deal on a presentation is very similar, and involves summarizing the key learning points, answering questions, reinforcing the relevance of the information, evaluating the session, and providing certificates to attendees. You should also provide your contact information in the event participants have difficulties implementing the new information, or to be used for referrals for future presentations.

Conducting dynamic meetings and presentations involves communication, preparation and creativity. Whether you present frequently or just when called upon to do so, the tips in this chapter will be beneficial to you. Ultimately, your success depends on you. You must possess the skills needed to make the presentation both informative and appealing to your audience. Do not be afraid to ask for assistance with developing materials or operating equipment. When your meeting or presentation is complete, you can consider it a success if your audience has gained new knowledge, skills or behaviors, or increased their awareness of a topic.

> *Know your stuff.*
> *Know whom you are stuffing.*
> *Know when they are stuffed.*
> —Dr. William Hendricks

Notes:

ABOUT THE AUTHOR

RIKI F. LOVEJOY-BLAYLOCK

Riki F. Lovejoy-Blaylock, is a returning author in the PWN Series, having completed her works in *Becoming the Professional Woman, The SuperWoman Syndrome* and her latest, *Women's Survival Guide for Overcoming Obstacles, Transition & Change.* Her experiences as a business owner in the male-dominated construction industry affords her the ability to talk from the heart about *Accepting Challenges.* Entering the construction industry in 1985 as a receptionist, Riki knew she wanted to be at the top some day. Her biggest challenges were finishing her education with two degrees taking night classes in between work travel and starting two separate businesses. It took over 20 years but Riki fully understands that the positive effects of her life today were due to the challenges accepted along the way.

Riki has worked for major general contractors in the Orlando, Florida market as a Project Manager and owned a carpentry subcontracting company in the early 90's. Currently Riki is the Executive Director for *RFL Consulting Solutions, LLC,* a construction management consulting firm, with management contracts on projects throughout the country. Her career has taken her to other parts of the world including BeiJing, People's Republic of China, Europe and the Caribbean.

Riki is a certified Minority Business Enterprise through the Florida Minority Suppliers Development Council as well as a certified Woman's Business Enterprise through the National Women Business Owners Corporation. Riki is continuously named to the Cambridge Who's Who of Business and Professional Executives and most recently was elected as the Region 3 Director for the National Association of Women In Construction, another long-time goal finally met after many challenges along the way!

Contact
Riki F. Lovejoy, Executive Director
RFL Consulting Solutions, LLC
5607 Bay Side Drive
Orlando, FL 32819-4046
Office: 407.443.3423
Fax: 407.612.6300
rlovejoy@rfl-consulting.com

SIX

ACCEPT THE CHALLENGE!

By Riki Lovejoy-Blaylock

"I have learned to be tenacious and less anxious about seeking help, as I've found everyone is willing to share advice and practical help. The biggest hindrance is self-doubt. Believe that you can do it – find solutions, and don't dwell on problems. And be prepared to take risks."
—Joyce Wilkinson (primary care nurse and Ph.D. student)

My mantra over the past few months has been, "Accept The Challenge Because You Are Very, Very Afraid." When I mentioned this to a friend of mine, she said, "What does that mean?" I looked at her and realized she had not been afraid enough lately and her life had become stagnant.

So what constitutes a challenge? We probably use this word on a somewhat daily basis. "Man, it's a challenge to get those kids to eat their broccoli!" or "Boy, she's got a challenge on her hands with that man!" The word "challenge" has become almost cliché. Yet, especially today, we need to understand the context of this word and what it means to the very core of our personal successes.

From Dictionary.com Unabridged (v 1.1), there are twenty-three definitions or uses of this word! There is the expected "a call to fight, as a battle, a duel, etc." and "a demand to explain, justify, etc." But the one that I really liked "difficulty in a job or undertaking that is STIMULATING to one engaged in it" pretty much explained it all to me because, you see for me, stimulation means fun, and I personally am at a point in my life that I want enjoyment. Also, I can look back on my life and realize that the real challenges I accepted really did make the road to today a bit more fun, although I probably didn't think so at the time!

And not to take away from the many challenges we may face on a day-to-day basis, especially as women, the challenges we need for our pleasure, for our personal successes, and for our continuous growth need to be the ones that we are afraid to face. So you are still asking, what is this woman talking about? Let's explore the challenges in our lives.

Facing The Challenges

In today's world we do have challenges that range from getting the kids to eat broccoli to what I believe is the most high of challenges – saving our very own life by dealing with a serious or terminal illness. And then there are those challenges in between, which are the continual shapers of who we are and who we want to be. And albeit much simpler, challenges start at a young age and tend to become harder as we grow older. You would think that with all the experience we may have had through our life's paths, it would be easier to face the challenges. But what kind of fun would it be to face only the easy stuff?

Let's look at the challenges we are facing at this point in our life. List five challenges you are facing today, in any order, and then rank them from 1 to 5, with 1 being the hardest challenge like a life-threatening illness and 5 being getting the men in your life to put the toilet seat down! You can have multiple rankings like Number 2 and Number 5 might be your 5's and Number 1 might be your Ranking 1. And let's date this list today. Be honest with yourself, and if you have more, use a separate sheet of paper.

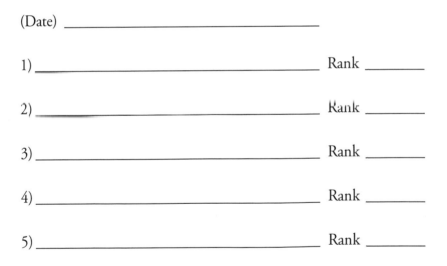

(Date) _____

1) _____ Rank _____

2) _____ Rank _____

3) _____ Rank _____

4) _____ Rank _____

5) _____ Rank _____

In evaluating the five (or more if you're like me!) challenges you are facing today, how many were the 4's or 5's? These are the ones that you can handle with no sweat! These are the everyday, gotta' do 'em, they are more of a pain in the you-know-where challenges that really aren't challenges, just another frustrating stressor added to your life's moments.

I pray you didn't have any 1's, or at the very least no more than one. Facing the challenge of a personal illness or that of a family member is definitely something you will be afraid of, and the journey to the final outcome will definitely be a life changing experience. But this is really for another chapter, another book!

Now let's look at those 2's and 3's. These are the challenges that may have been presented to you that you say, "Oh gosh, I don't know how to do that" or "I can't do that", yet you have no choice but to do it for various reasons, like it has to be done and there's no one else to do it, or you are *afraid* you might lose your job if you don't do it! If you'll notice, when I was giving you the instruction for listing your challenges, I didn't give you a description of what to list per se, nor explain the 2's and 3's rankings, and yet you probably have them on your list. These are in your subconscious mind as a challenge and not as a task that you may do on a daily basis. Maybe for you, doing a presentation to a group of 50 peers is not a challenge because you have now done it everyday for the last five years and it didn't show up on this list. But what is on your list is the presentation you were asked to do before an assembly of the 1,000-member organization, Women Having Associative Challenges and Kicking Overbearing Spouses (aka WHACKOS). So what's the challenge? A presentation is a presentation! What is the fear you are facing with this challenge? Will you do the WHACKOS presentation because you are afraid or will you not do the presentation because you are afraid? Your answer should be you will definitely do the presentation because you are afraid, but know you will become the better, stronger person for doing this, regardless of what the WHACKOS think!

In a paper written by Michael S. Brockman from the University of California, Davis and Stephen T. Russell, Ph.D. from the University of Arizona, they write that studies of middle and high school students that chose diverse and challenging activities were more persistent in achieving their goals; they were said to have initiative. Reed W. Larson from the University of Illinois at Urbana-Champaign and author/co-editor of *The Changing Adolescent Experience*, defines initiative as the motivation to direct effort toward achieving challenging goals and remain determined, even when things get difficult. In the context of Mr. Larson's description, he is referring to youth, but this definition is so eloquent and applicable to our adult life. Essentially, the students who were said to have initiative go on to become life-long learners. They become more confident that their own lives are in their control and their environment becomes what they want it to be. Isn't that where we want to be as confident, successful women? **I say, if the kids can do it, by gosh women can be the best at it.**

Facing Your Challenge or Facing Your Fears?

There is a very fine line between whether you are facing the challenge presented to you or if you are facing an internal fear. The challenge becomes a challenge because you are afraid of some aspect of the challenge. Remember the presentation to the WHACKOS? Why was this a challenge but the 50-person peer presentation was not? Is there a 'fear factor' that changes the dynamics of the WHACKOS presentation, such as the large group (the numbers), or the anonymity of the women, or even just the make-up of the organization; I mean after all, who really wants to speak before a group of WHACKOS?

Let's look at your list of challenges again that you made earlier, but this time let's look at it as to WHY it's a challenge. Is it a challenge because it's an everyday, tedious task, or is there a 'fear' associated with it? If you have a 1-ranked challenge, there is no doubt a fear associated with it. Please write that specific fear. Again, we are not going to address it much with this chapter, but we need to still recognize the fears associated with challenges.

Challenge	Fear
1)	
2)	
3)	
4)	
5)	

Okay, we now know what you are *afraid* of! These challenges that are on your list are obviously ones that you've already said yes to. You've been presented the challenge by others and have said yes, or you presented this challenge to yourself and have accepted that you will meet the challenge! Good for you! You're continuing your journey to personal growth.

But what about those fears that we've now made you look at? What are we going to do with them? We are going to face them! The challenge cannot be accomplished without facing the fear. Without your continued growth happening, you will become stagnant. The bad news is there is no magic available to help you get past the fear. The only way you can do it is the Nike way – Just Do It! What we can do is look at the ramifications of accepting the challenge.

Look Within.

Women have an innate sense of instinct. You may have heard about it, 'women's intuition'. Although you may have accepted any given challenge kickin' and screamin', you subconsciously accepted the challenge because your gut instinct assured you you could do it before you verbally said yes. Once you consciously said yes, your self-doubt took over and started reminding you that you were afraid. Amazing what damage self-doubt does, but guess what . . . the subconscious is more amazing and stronger, if we let it be. As I state in my chapter, *Setting Goals for Success*, in the book *Women's Survival Guide for Overcoming Obstacles, Transition & Change*, the subconscious mind is an incredible part of our being. Scientific studies have proven how the subconscious can and will define our actions, and ultimately define what we will become. Based on his 20 year study of what made people successful, Earl Nightingale, the late "Creator of the Self-Improvement Industry" finally claimed – *we become what we think about!* So we work our challenge to a successful end when we give in to our instinct and our subconscious, which knew all along that we could do it. The added bonus is that each time you accept a challenge and complete it to its successful end, you have added another notch to your confidence level. Your courage is increased and with each challenge presented to you, it is a little easier to say yes.

So Why Do I Want to Accept the Challenge?

Of course, what you don't want is to accept challenges that don't present a challenge to you. You've heard it all before, read it in a kazillion self-help articles, and know instinctively ... you need to step out of your comfort zone! If the challenge is comfortable for you, it's really more of a task, not something from which you will learn and grow. The challenge you accept that takes you out of your comfort zone, which you will succeed with and build your confidence and courage, is the one that will take you places beyond your wildest dream, if you want it to! If your wildest dream is to preach to a stadium filled with 10,000 people, then you have to present to a crowd of 1,000 WHACKOS! Because it will be at this presentation that you will gain the knowledge of how to present to a large crowd, or how to overcome the fact that you do not know a single face in the crowd, or that it doesn't matter one iota that someone didn't like your presentation. Preaching to 10,000 people is living your dream.

What Are My Gains? What Are My Losses?

Accepting challenges really exhibits a snowball effect, which in the end means success for you. So what am I saying? We've already said that accepting challenges and bringing it to a successful conclusion will build your confidence. There is also a tangible reality to accepting challenges – you will build skills, you will build reputation, you will build knowledge and ultimately, you could be building your big fat retirement account!

With each challenge comes a realization that, first it is a challenge and secondly, you have to figure out why it is a challenge. (Remember, it's only a challenge if it presents a challenge, like a need for a skill you've never used before.) What is your self-doubt telling you you can't do? Let me be the first to tell you that it's not that you can't do it; it's just that you've never done it before. Here's a totally cliché statement for you – Step Out of Your Comfort Zone and Just Do It!

So, now you've accomplished the challenge. What did you gain? Perhaps it was another skill. Maybe you weren't efficient in the use of a particular software application, but because the boss said this was the future of the company and you need your job, you tackle that software package with a vengeance. In short time, you amaze even yourself as you've now not only become proficient, but you are also dubbed 'the guru'. Whew! Challenge accomplished, you're feeling gooooodddd! What did you gain – a new skill, a reputation – not only that you're 'the guru', but that the boss now sees you as a woman that gets things done! What did you lose? Maybe a few hairs from pulling it out as you have one (or more) frustrating moments during the learning process; you've lost the ability to say 'no' when someone asks for your help, because you know it all now and hopefully, you lost the fear you previously 'pegged' to this challenge that you didn't know what you were doing! I'd say that loss is a 'gain' – what about you?

Here comes the snowball… Act II - the boss comes back to you, pats you on the back, and tells you what a great job you did. He also reminds you this software application is the future of the company, which has offices around the Southeast Region of the United States. You've done such a wonderful job with this, how about teaching all the others that haven't figured it out yet?? And oh by the way, trainers get double the salary you're making now and some extra perks. Yikes! What do you say? You've barely traveled outside your home state, and definitely not so much by plane, yet the idea of the travel and visiting other places excites you, and who wouldn't want to double their salary?? You say yes, of course!

What are your gains – more money, more perks, you find that you love to travel, you get to spend some time in some fascinating cities that you probably couldn't or wouldn't have on your 'old' salary (and the company is paying for you to be there!) and you're able to start socking some money away for retirement. What are your losses? Time away from home, family and friends, having to deal with TSA at the airports, and probably some lost luggage, if you do this work long enough. This time the evaluation of the gain versus the loss is a bit more significant. What are you willing to sacrifice when you make your decision on this challenge? There are times when the gain is not worth it to you, if the losses are too important. Each person's circumstances play a huge part in accepting challenges, and even though you may be tempted to accept this challenge for the gains, your first instinct may be to say NO! Of course, you need to weigh the gains and losses as well for a no response. Either way, trust that your first instinct knows the right answer. Today this challenge is the road to choose; next year it may not!

I had an Act II decision to make not long ago. I had a contract that kept me away from home 8 to 10 weeks at a time, and I ended up being gone a total of 9 months out of 12. I was an experienced traveler, so that wasn't the issue, but my 'fear' that my self-doubt conjured up was whether I would be effective in the scope of work to which I was contracting. Of course, I had not ever stayed at resorts in Myrtle Beach, Vail, or Maui so this was an immediate "gain" for me. Tough gig, eh?? Additionally, the contract was quite lucrative for me, and for the first year of the contract, my life and the other contracts I had in place allowed for me to be away. Even my husband was good with me making this decision. But a year later, the decision to re-up the contract was with totally different life circumstances, and my gut said – No More. Today I know it was the right decision. I picked up so much (really too much) more work that it more than made up for the contract I gave up, and I get to be home with my husband, family and friends.

Accepting the challenge is, ultimately, about knowing and understanding your inner self – believing your first instinct – that gut feeling. It's about knowing what your self-doubt keeps you from doing, and it's knowing that you can do anything. Keep accepting the challenges for the gains, and even the losses. Keep accepting the challenges for the stimulation and fun that you will experience along the way. Keep Accepting the Challenges Because You Are Very Afraid!

Winners Are People Like You
Winners take chances.
Like everyone else, they fear failing,
But they refuse to let fear control them.
Winners don't give up.
When life gets rough, they hang in until the going gets better.
Winners are flexible.
They realize there is more than one way and are willing to try others.
Winners know they are not perfect.
They respect their weaknesses while making the most of their strengths.
Winners fall, but they don't stay down.
They stubbornly refuse to let a fall keep them from climbing.
Winners don't blame fate for their failures, not luck for their successes.
Winners accept responsibility for their lives.
Winners are positive thinkers who see good in all things.
From the ordinary, they make the extraordinary.
Winners believe in the path they have chosen, even when it's hard,
Even when others can't see where they are going.
Winners are patient.
They know a goal is only as worthy as the effort that's required to achieve it.
Winners are people like you.
They make this world a better place to be.
—Nancye Sims

ABOUT THE AUTHOR

AHMON`DRA (BRENDA) McCLENDON

Ahmon`dra, President of Brilliance Inc., is an international speaker, facilitator, motivator and author. She imprints an indelible impression upon your heart and makes you smile, laugh, cry and contemplate the deeper issues of life. She arouses in each listener a passion to commit to his or her higher purpose with her grace, power and spirit.

With twenty plus years in the human services arena and an MSW from San Francisco State University, Ahmon`dra has developed a highly successful program called P.L.A.N.E. – "Passionately Living A New Existence." She has spoken to thousands of young adults in North America, Europe and Africa on how to create a powerful future by staying devoted to their dreams, trusting their intuition, boldly taking risks and asking for what they want.

She is a Certified Facilitator for Motivating the Teen Spirit Inc. a teen empowerment program that conducts transformational workshops, and leads the international program, Core Value Training as a Senior Instructor. Ahmon`dra is a recipient of the "Speaking with an Active Voice" grant sponsored by the American Medical Women's Association and Pharmacia Corporation.

A contributing author to the best selling book *Chicken Soup For the African-American Soul*, she was featured as a keynote speaker for The Monster Diversity 2003 Leadership Program in the United States.

Passion and magnificence exude from her presence with an amazing energy of wisdom, healing & love as she creates, flies and soars! Get clear on your life and passions with the energy and excitement of Ahmon`dra

Contact
Ahmon`dra (Brenda) McClendon
Brilliance, Inc.
484 Lakepark Ave pmb 485
Oakland, California 94610
Ahmondra@aol.com
www.protrain.net

SEVEN

MENTORING AND EMPOWERING YOUNG PEOPLE

By Ahmon'dra McClendon

U nlike any other generation, today's youth are faced with an unprecedented array of life challenges. Technology has condensed their world to a few keystrokes and placed everything at their fingertips. Most young people today don't have the mental and emotional capacity to grasp the complex issues they are dealing with, and as a result, they are stressed out. Because of the added pressures, mentoring and empowering young people is especially crucial during this century. Almost from the moment they are born, young people are confronted with adult challenges.

"Authorities in St. Petersburg, Florida shackled both the wrists and ankles of one five-year-old child and removed her from school after she had quieted down from a 30-minute temper tantrum."

As parents, educators, and providers, it is our obligation and responsibility to protect our youth and prepare them for success. This becomes more difficult as the dangers they face not only lurk outside their homes, but also enter into the privacy of their bedrooms via the Internet.

"Federal authorities believe that at least 500,000 to 750,000 predators are "on-line" on a daily basis, constantly combing through these blog sites...looking for their ideal victim."

"Pornographers disguise their sites (i.e. "stealth" sites) with common brand names, including Disney, Barbie, ESPN, etc., to entrap children."

Young people are up close and personal with trauma on a daily basis. They are in imminent danger of being shot just by walking down the street. Their reality is, the world is an unsafe place.

The number of children and teens killed by gun violence in 2003 alone exceeds the number of American fighting men and women killed in hostile action in Iraq from 2003 to April 2006." (Children's Defense Fund)

We can't protect our youth from every unsafe circumstance they may confront. But we can empower them to be strong individuals, capable of sorting through the myriad of choices available to them. As mentors, we must guide, direct and empower young people to meet the challenges of today.

Each day in America:
　5 children or teens commit suicide.
　192 children are arrested for violent crimes.
　1,153 babies are born to teen mothers.
　2,261 high school students drop out.
　4,302 children are arrested.
　17,132 public school students are suspended.

It is not enough to teach youth phrases such as, "just say no", or provide them with safe houses to run to. Young people must have the mental capability to distinguish between what is good and what is harmful to them. They need to make quick sound decisions based on facts, not fiction. This requires abstract thinking, and abstract thinking calls for "emotional stability".

Emotional stability is having a cluster of beliefs, behaviors, and attitudes that, when used together, create mental healthiness and empowerment. When young people are emotionally *unhealthy,* they are incapable of utilizing mentoring or developing inner strength. Their confusion prevents them from seeing the bigger picture and reaching logical conclusions. When they are emotionally healthy, they develop the self-confidence to make sound life decisions.

Lisa Nichols, teacher of "*The Secret*" and CEO, founder of "Motivating The Teen Spirit," instructs that the success of empowering young people depends on creating a program that teaches and supports emotional stability.

The premise of The MTS program is that when teens are emotionally healthy, they make integrity-based decisions through self-love, and their uniqueness is expressed in positive behaviors. They are receptive to new information and more empowered to express unconditional love to others.

Working with youth in the 21st century requires a new course of action. Using outdated turn-of-the-century rules and regulations to mentor our teens does them a disservice. We must begin developing our future leaders today.

In this chapter, techniques and strategies for effective mentoring will be outlined, along with examples of how empowerment develops from emotional healthiness.

Road Map to Mentoring

Successful mentoring rests on a foundation of emotional stability. When young people are emotionally clear, their capacity for reasoning increases and they become teachable. Programs containing strategies and techniques that foster emotional healthiness are successful because they help teens develop self-awareness. Young people with insight into their behaviors are more receptive to change.

Foster Empowerment—Strategy #1

Mentors must refrain from telling young people what to do, and create safe spaces for them to practice decision-making. When they experience different consequences as a result of their decision-making, young people become empowered and gain the ability to address their problems.

> **Being Empowered Produces Self-Discipline, Autonomy Respect, Honesty, And Emotional Healthiness**

Controlled Chaos Technique

When working with teens, always maintain an atmosphere of fairness, safety and direction. Teens like to know what is expected of them.

- Use written or verbal contracts - they teach the importance of honoring your word.

- Create guidelines - they clearly define appropriate and non-appropriate behaviors.

- Make agreements - they allow for free choice with consequences. (If you accept the agreements you can stay, if not, you can leave and deal with the consequences.)

Never use rules to control an environment; they set up a hierarchy of authority and automatically put teens at a disadvantage.

Exercise

You are preparing to establish mentoring groups.

a.   Compose a contract to use with a group of seniors in H.S.

b.   Develop a set of guidelines to use with a girl's group.

c.   Create four agreements to use with a youth church group.

Build Trust—Strategy #2

The basis of mentoring is trust. It is important to first establish trust, and then provide guidance and direction. Always ask yourself the question: What is the best way to build trust? Don't make the mistake of judging teens by their behaviors. *Their looks can be deceiving*!

Trust produces
Self-Expression-Empathy-Integrity
Emotional Healthiness + Empowerment

The Quiet Approach Technique

In a workshop, a young man sat with his head down, hood over his head, arms folded and back to me. From all appearances, he was asleep. I never asked him to change his posture. At the end of the day, he stood up, removed his hood, and announced to the group that when he came in he was feeling depressed and on edge (angry enough to hurt someone) because his mother had been arrested for drugs the night before. After being in our session, he felt better because he was able to just sit, listen and get positive support from his peers.

Suppose I had tried to force him to take his hood off, sit up straight, face me and interact with the group. What do you think the outcome would have been? What approach would you have used in this situation?

Cultivate Independence—Strategy #3

"Teach, don't Preach" is my motto. The most powerful tool in mentoring is "sharing". When teens hear life stories of struggles and triumphs, they learn by example. They develop the mental ability to draw conclusions and make behavioral changes independently. Lessons based on real life challenges promote growth.

> **Independence produces**
> **Discernment-Self-Examination-Courage-Independent Thinking**
> **Emotional Healthiness + Empowerment**

Jazz It Up! The 21st Century Delivery System Technique

Our teens live in a multi-media world. The most effective way to deliver lessons is using a multi-media approach.

- Use Music to Set the Tone. Are you teaching a lesson on increasing self-esteem building? Find an artist (teens admire) with a powerful message and use their CD to enhance the lesson. Set the tone while teens are working by playing music in the background. You can lower the energy level in a room just by playing music.

- Use Videos and DVD's. Show a 3 – 5 minute clip from a DVD showing how a celebrity made it against all odds. Help teens to make the connections between the "bling bling" of a celebrity's life and the real day-to-day struggles. Putting things in perspective helps them to see life more realistically. (All that glitters isn't gold.)

- Use PowerPoint Presentations. Why use chalk on the board when you can design a moving, singing, dancing, and humorous presentation that will catch and hold their attention.

- Use Movement. Design lessons that require physical movement. Have everyone blow up five balloons and label them with positive traits. Let them exchange balloons by hitting them to a partner. Teens spend all day sitting in chairs in classrooms. You want to distinguish your sessions from the classroom.

- Use the Lecture Format Sparingly. Young people learn from each other so put them together.

  1. Place teens in small group setting. (Circles)

  2. Let teens work together in pairs.

  3. Use a student to co-teach with you.

Creating a relaxing, fun, engaging and learning environment is mandatory for mentoring today's youth. **Think of your delivery system as modes of transportation.** Do your lessons travel by:

Horse and carriage – slow and rocky

Foot – slow, steady, and gets tired real fast

Bus – moderate pace and stops often

Car – can move slow, moderate or fast, but can only carry a few passengers

Plane – fast speed, goes far, carries many passengers, shows movies, has food, provides accommodations for all, (shy students, overachievers, educationally challenged), uses a variety of staff, is fun and exciting

Exercise

1. Find five recording artists that deliver powerful positive messages that young people relate to.

2. Create five lessons that require physical movement.

3. Write a five-minute skit on empowerment for teens to perform.

Answer "Unasked" Questions—Strategy #4

Young people live in a world of unanswered questions. They don't always know what to ask, but they know they need answers. It is our responsibility to help them identify the questions and find the answers. Sometime the best way to provide answers is by sharing our experiences.

Openness produces
Self-Expression-Trust-Non-Judgment
Emotional Healthiness + Empowerment

Tell-All Session Technique

Ask me anything? Creating sessions where teens have the freedom to ask you anything opens the door for powerful dialogue. When teens learn that I grew up in public housing and had to fight to survive in my neighborhood, they learn a powerful lesson on judgment. Just because I look and sound a certain way doesn't mean I didn't have the same challenges. The best way to teach openness is to model it.

Exercise

1. Write down five questions you are uncomfortable answering in front of a group of teens. As a mentor, you must be willing to step out of your comfort zone and teach lessons from your life experiences.

2. Conduct a self-inventory and ask yourself why you're uncomfortable answering those questions?

Effective Mentoring

Working with young people is fun, exciting, rewarding, and sometimes unnerving. A mentor's biggest challenge is deciding how to handle a particular situation. A good rule of thumb to use is to always concentrate on creating empowerment.

A Young woman who was anorexic and drug addicted completed both her programs successfully. When she started to lose weight, everyone suspected she was active in her addictions again. She was adamant that she was eating and not using drugs. Her drug test was negative, so it was concluded that it must be her anorexia. Even though the evidence was stacked against her, I continued to believe in and support her. One day she got violently sick in school and was rushed to emergency. They discovered her gallbladder needed to be removed. That was the reason for her weight lost. She was telling the truth all along. Believing in young people when all the evidence is against them is difficult, but sometimes necessary.

****

While conducting a workshop in a large juvenile detention facility, I noticed a very angry looking young man sitting alone. I approached him and asked if I could work with him. He had no reason to trust me or interact with me, but he agreed. During the exercise, he shared with me that sometimes he just wanted a "hug". At the end of the exercise, with his permission, I gave him a hug, and asked why he chose to work with me. He said he felt respected when I asked him and didn't tell him to work with me. And when he looked into my eyes, he saw no judgment. Remember, every young person needs unconditional love, no matter what their circumstances are.

The African Proverb, "It takes a village to raise a child" is more true today than any other time in history. The resources we once enjoyed (big extended families, helping neighbors, next-door teen baby sitters) have all but vanished, and families are struggling to just provide day-to-day care for their children. The statistics for the youth in this country show that they are at risk.

"9.9% of 16 to 19-year-olds are not enrolled in school and are not high school graduates.

The High school completion rate is 85.7%.

16.5% of 16 to 19-year-olds are unemployed. (Children's Defense Fund)

The current trends will stop when young people are given the guidance and direction they need. All adults have to be accountable, whether they work directly with young people or not. It is imperative that we re-create that global village and start building our future leaders today.

Be a mentor to a teen. They need it, and we owe it to them.

Resorces
Children's Defense Fund
25 E Street, NW
Washington, DC 20001
(202) 628-8787
www.Childrensdefense.org

Lisa Nichols, CEO and Founder of 'Motivating the Teen Spirit'
www.motivatingtheteenspirit.com

ABOUT THE AUTHOR

ROSEMARY MEDEL

A City Planner for the last seventeen years in Southern California, Rosemary has worked for the cities of Huntington Beach, Cypress and Signal Hill. A Bachelor of Fine Arts degree with an emphasis in Environmental Design, California State University at Fullerton has prepared Ms. Medel for her current profession in Land Use Planning. She feels strongly about giving back to her community and has volunteered her Planning expertise to the community where she currently resides. Rosemary is a former Planning Commissioner for the City of La Habra where she assisted in guiding development during her three-year term. Currently, Rosemary is a Realtor, and is the owner and president of The Medel Group. Her firm is committed to training and preparing its clients facing risks with confidence, develop their professional image through improved public speaking and presentation skills. She is a co-author of *You're on Stage! Image, Etiquette, Branding & Style, Emotional Wellness for Women: Mind Body & Spirit, Survival Guide for Overcoming Obstacles, Transition & Change, Women as Leaders* and slated to co-author future PWN books titled, *Beyond the Body! Developing Inner Beauty, Young Man's Guide for Personal Success,* and *The Baby Boomer's Handbook for Women.*

Rosemary is a certified trainer in Woman's Issues and a certified Professional Coach and is an International Advisory Board member of the Professional Woman Network. She is also a member of both The Professional Woman Network International Speakers Bureau and the National Association of Female Executives. Rosemary is available for personal and professional coaching sessions.

Her most important role and accomplishment has been raising her two grown children Rosalie and Eli.

Contact
Rosemary Medel
The Medel Group
P.O. Box 2204
La Habra, CA 90632-2204
rosemedel@juno.com
www.TheMedelGroup.com

EIGHT

SEXUAL HARASSMENT

By Rosemary Medel

Discrimination based on sex includes sexual harassment, gender harassment, and harassment based on pregnancy, childbirth, or medical conditions related to pregnancy or childbirth. The state I live in is California; therefore, the laws I will speak to relate to California. (However, your state may have similar laws, since most laws adopted by states will be based on Federal law and statutes). The information discussed in this chapter is available online, at your place of employment, and by contacting your particular State resources. For disclosure purposes, let me emphasize that **I AM NOT AN ATTORNEY.** For advice on a pending claim, please contact an attorney or contact the U.S. Equal Employment Opportunity Commission *(see end of chapter for contact information).*

Like every other woman on the planet, I have my own sexual harassment stories! However, I would venture to guess that the majority of a woman's sexual harassment experiences have occurred outside the work place. But right now, let's discuss your protection rights in the work environment. The definition of sexual harassment as defined by the Fair Employment and Housing Act (FEHA) states that sexual harassment includes many forms of offensive behavior, including harassment of a person of same gender as the harasser. The following is a partial list of types of sexual harassment:

- Unwanted sexual advances

- Offering employment benefits in exchange for sexual favors

- Actual or threatened retaliation

- Leering; making sexual gestures; or displaying sexually suggestive objects, pictures, cartoons, or posters

- Making or using derogatory comments, epithets, slurs, or jokes

- Sexual comments, including graphic comments about an individual's body; sexually degrading words used to describe an individual; or suggestive or obscene letters, notes, or invitations

- Physical touching or assault, as well as impeding or blocking movements

State law has covered an array of situations that could potentially be offensive to a person. But the key is, **what is offensive to one person may not be to another**. Of the list formulated by the State of California, identify what would not be offensive to you.

- _____

- _____
- _____
- _____

Behavior in our society is influenced by music and movies and has certainly changed how people (especially women) are treated. We as women need to take responsibility for how we allow men to treat us based on our perception of ourselves. This self-image will carry with you throughout your work career and into all your relationships. You must decide when someone has crossed the line into the realm of sexual harassment. Your responsibility is however, to be consistent in your behavior. What does this mean? As a woman, you are sending a message to others of the opinion you have of yourself by the manner in which you dress, speak, conduct yourself in public, and how you treat others. Does this make sense? In essence, you are setting the bar. This list of do's and don'ts is my advice to young women entering the work force and advice I gave to my daughter Rosalie growing up.

What to Wear and How to Act Do's and Don'ts

1. Do not wear anything in which you are not prepared to handle comments (i.e. low-cut necklines, tight cloths, short clothes, etc.).

2. If you are to uncomfortable to sneeze in that skirt or dress, it's too short.

3. Do not dress for work the same way you would dress for a club.

4. Leave the killer high heels for after work.

5. If you want to be taken seriously as a woman wanting to move up at work based on your work ethic and merit, then dress the part!

Now, there may always be someone who wants to challenge your standards to see if you are a person of integrity or if you will deviate from your standards. Let them try. It will not change who you are unless you allow the change. Strength to speak up for yourself comes from knowing who you are, knowing what you want, and from being a mentally mature, strong woman. Each woman will react differently to sexual harassment, based on her life experiences, religious beliefs, or personal values. One's perception of any given situation can be assessed by no other means. So, how do you determine if you are being harassed of just being too sensitive?

Perception

Let me give you an example. When I was about six years old, I was at a restaurant with my mother and she was speaking with a male friend of hers. I was seated between them. This man had not seen me in a long time, and was taken with me. He told my mother that I was so pretty, and proceeded to place his hand on top of my little hand. While she was taking in the compliment, I felt my space invaded. I was embarrassed and started to cry. My mother was surprised at my reaction, and told me that he was just complimenting me. That was no compliment to me! He was touching my hand. It just didn't feel right. This was my **PERCEPTION!** So, at six years old I did not have the skills to respond to anyone making me feel uncomfortable. I can assure you that I have come a long way, baby! But, it was through life experiences that I learned to stand up for myself. I received a lot of attention growing up because of my appearance, as do most women. Some attention was complimentary, others by today's definition, were harassment.

As a woman, someone is always evaluating your appearance. We however, determine when someone has crossed the line from compliment to harassment. I would guess that one inappropriate comment is not going to send you over the edge. Let's create a list of your experiences. What has been your experience with people crossing the line?

- _____
- _____
- _____
- _____
- _____
- _____
- _____
- _____

How did you handle these various situations?

- _____
- _____
- _____

- _____
- _____
- _____
- _____
- _____

As we all know and have experienced, women tolerate a lot of harassment in different forms. As a strong woman, you may want to confront the harasser immediately to stop the behavior. In fact, I would think that they would be shocked that you stood up for yourself. In my opinion, a person who is a habitual harasser is a bully. They prey on the weak, the young, and the inexperienced. If you have tried to confront the harasser and nothing else is working, this is your **Plan B**.

Filing a Complaint

In the work environment, if you believe you have a sexual harassment complaint, you can first speak with your immediate supervisor. Ok, what if your supervisor is doing the harassment? By right, you may speak with any supervisor or director in your organization. You can even bypass them and go directly to Human Resources (HR) to file a complaint. By this action, you have now started the process of confronting the harasser in a formal setting that will expose their behavior. Remember that you must make sure HR is doing their job to protect your rights. Ask lots of questions regarding the process.

One way that a company or organizations protects themselves from being involved in potential lawsuits, thereby avoiding liability, is to provide a training program to prevent harassment. Or, once aware of any harassment, the employer takes immediate and appropriate corrective action to stop the harassment. The process to stop any harassment in the work place always begins with your employer. Once you notify your employer of the complaint, they will do the following:

1. Investigate the complaint.

2. Review the information gathered through the investigation.

3. Report their determination to harasser, supervisor or department head.

4. Take reasonable steps to protect you from further harassment.

5. Take reasonable steps to protect you from retaliation.

You also have the right to report your complaint to an outside Administrative Agency, like the U.S. Department of Equal Opportunity Commission (EEOC). This is a Federal Agency. Or you can file your complaint with your particular state under Fair Employment and Housing.

You have **one year** from the time of harassment to file a complaint of discrimination with the Department of Fair Employment & Housing. The Fair Employment Agency serves as a fact finding neutral party attempting to help the parties voluntarily resolve disputes. If they find sufficient evidence to establish discrimination occurred and settlement efforts fail, the Department may file a formal accusation. The accusation will lead to either a public hearing before the Fair Employment and Housing Commission, or a lawsuit filed by the DFEH on behalf of the complaining party. If the Commission finds that discrimination has occurred, it can order remedies including:

- Fines or damages for emotional distress from each employer or person found to have violated the law

- Hiring or reinstatement

- Back pay or promotion

- Changes in the policies or practices of the involved employer

Employees can also pursue the matter though a private lawsuit in civil court, after a complaint has been filed with DFEH and Right-to-Sue Notice has been issued.

If you are starting your own business, then one of the things you will learn is about employer's obligations to address sexual harassment and discrimination. Your responsibility as an employer is as follows:

- Take reasonable steps to prevent discrimination and harassment from occurring.

- Develop and implement a sexual harassment prevention program and policy with a procedure for employees to make complaints, and for employers to investigate complaints.

- Take prompt and effective corrective action if the harassment allegations are proven.

- Post the Department of Fair Employment and Housing employment post in the workplace.

- Distribute an information sheet on sexual harassment to all employees.

- All employees should be made aware of the seriousness of violations of the sexual harassment policy. Supervisory personnel should be educated about their specific responsibilities. All employees must be cautioned against using peer pressure to discourage harassment victims from complaining.

This information is all online. EEOC Contact information: National Contact Center (NCC) customer service representatives are available to assist you in more than 100 languages between 8:00 a.m. and 8:00 p.m. Eastern Time. An automated system with answers to frequently asked questions is available on a 24-hour basis. You can reach the NCC:

By mail:
U.S. Equal Employment Opportunity Commission
P.O. Box 7033
Lawrence, Kansas 66044

Or, by phone:
1-800-669-4000

ABOUT THE AUTHOR

VIVA L MCCARVER

Mrs. Viva McCarver is the President and primary consultant of Viva McCarver & Associates a personal and professional development training company located in Toledo, Ohio. The goal of the company is to form partnering relationships with churches, organizations and school systems providing unique training solutions that will promote enhancement, retention and upward mobility. Viva has over 14 years of experience in the area of Human Resource Management. Her expertise includes, but is not limited to counseling; benefits administration, recruitment, salary administration, training & development; policy development; leadership development and motivational speaking.

Mrs. McCarver earned a Masters Degree in Leadership & Organizational Development and a Bachelor's Degree in Business Management from The University of Findlay. She also holds a Bachelor of Science Degree in Business Management and an Associates Degree in Business Administration. She is also a certified trainer and a member of The Professional Woman Network an international training organization.

Viva has had many years of experience in the area of Management which has provided her with a strong aptitude to lead and inspire others in developing their overall personal and professional aspirations. She believes that success starts from within so it is essential to have the necessary skills developed on the inside of you in order to thrive to your supreme altitude of greatness.

In her spare time she enjoys reading, shopping and traveling but most of all she enjoys being able to share her life with those she cherish the most, her family and friends.

Contact:
Viva McCarver & Associates
P.O. Box 6469
Toledo, Ohio 43612
(419) 377-6233
Email: vmccarver@buckeye-express.com
Website: www.protrain.net

NINE

10 STRATEGIES FOR INCREASED SELF-ESTEEM

By Viva McCarver

Throughout your life you go through different experiences, both good and bad, that have some type of impact on you. Those experiences create the individual feelings and thoughts that you tend to develop about yourself over time, which ultimately affect your self-esteem. So we ask the question; "what is self-esteem"? "Do I have high or low self-esteem"? As you research the term, you will find that there are many different definitions available. The Webster dictionary defines it as: *a confidence and satisfaction in oneself.* If you are the type of person that constantly puts yourself down, or always blame others and never take responsibility, you could be suffering from low self-esteem. In contrast, if you are someone who has confidence and self-respect, you would be considered to have high self-esteem.

Low self-esteem is a problem that many people face. It can be triggered by different factors, such as stress, treatment from others, failures and fears. The way you feel about yourself has a major influence on your mind, body and behavior. For example, if you constantly tell yourself that you are a failure, then there is a good chance that you will never believe that you can accomplish anything. If a parent constantly tells a child that he or she is stupid, then it can probably be expected for that child to receive bad grades because this is what they have come to believe.

Well, the good news is that if you are suffering from low self-esteem, it can be changed. You can take back your life and find your true value. You can begin to love yourself again. You can begin to smile again. If you want it, you can have it! Throughout this chapter you will find ten key strategies to get you back to a life full of joy and happiness.

1. Believe in Yourself.

To believe in anything is often a challenge for most people. The world seems to be filled with so much corruption and lies that we tend to become skeptical of everything that we hear on the television, radio, or even in person. But often I wonder why people don't at least believe in themselves. Is it because of past experiences, lack of confidence or fear? Honestly, it's probably a combination of them all. Our belief system is developed early in childhood. We believe that our parents will take care of us forever. We believe that we will never get hurt, and we feel that we can do anything because we will always have the support. Well, as you go through life you begin to realize that it doesn't necessarily happen the way that you had envisioned. For some people, going through different experiences in life has damaged their personal belief system.

When you stop believing in yourself, you basically allow negative things to take place in your life. If you have been beaten, you refuse to fight back. If you are verbally insulted, you will not respond. You initially develop an "I don't care" attitude.

Well, it's time to take charge of your life. Start believing in yourself again. Regain the self-respect and dignity that you once had. Become a leader in every aspect of your life. It's not always easy to get back to where you use to be, but start by telling yourself these three things on a daily basis

1. I am powerful and can do anything that I put my mind to.

2. I will stand up for what I believe.

3. I deserve to live a happy and prosperous life.

If you don't believe in something, you will fall for anything!

2. Improve Your Skills

As human beings, we have all been blessed with a gift or talent at which we are exceptional; but we must remember there is always room for improvement. You should always have the desire and ambition to improve in the areas in which you are weak, and continue to strengthen the areas in which you are strong. For example, when I started working in the corporate world, there were many opportunities that passed me by because I was not qualified. I then realized that in order for me to grow, it would be my responsibility to make it happen. I decided to go back to school to get my college degree. Through my own self-initiative, I received my BA in Business Management and a MBA in Leadership and Organizational Development. Attending college enhanced my knowledge and skills, and it also gave me the self-confidence that I needed to advance in my career.

To look at it from a different aspect, let's focus on a professional basketball player. In order to maintain and enhance their abilities, he or she must condition and practice on a daily or weekly basis. For example, if they are weak at shooting foul shots, then they will practice shooting 50 to 100 fouls shots a day to get better. If they choose not to practice, then they will never get to the next level and their performance will remain the same.

Improving your skills will make you a better person. You will become more satisfied with your life. You will be more willing to take chances and experience new things, which will build your self-confidence. Ultimately, you will begin to focus on what you can do rather than what you cannot.

3. Learn How To Forgive.

Forgiveness is one of the most difficult things to do. We often look at forgiveness as something that is earned. For example, if your best friend took something from you, your first initial thought is that he or she needs to come to you and apologize before you even entertain the thought of forgiving them. The truth is, forgiveness is something that we must learn to do for **ourselves**. When you forgive, you don't do it for the other person, you do it for YOU!

Forgiveness is a choice. When you choose to hold on to past hurts and pains, you will never be able to move on with your life. Those past experiences are like cancer in the body, and it continues to spread until it has consumed your whole life. One false impression about forgiveness is that, if you choose to forgive, you are overlooking the act that has happened. This is not true! It simply means that you acknowledge the act, and that you will not remain a victim of the circumstance. It means that you have found peace and tranquility, and that you are willing to move on.

Forgiveness is the key to raising self-esteem. It removes the anger, resentment and self-pity from your life. It allows you be free and happy. It restores your confidence and faith within yourself. Learning how to forgive is not easy, but it is well worth it!

"When you hold resentment toward another, you are bound to that person or condition by an emotional link that is stronger than steel. Forgiveness is the only way to dissolve that link and get free." —Catherine Ponder

4. Live a Prayerful Life.

Prayer is powerful! Prayer changes lives! If you don't already say a daily prayer, I would encourage you to do so. The Bible says in Matthew 21:22, *"All things, whatsoever you shall ask in prayer, believing, you shall receive."* When you pray, you are relying on God's power to transform you. It's a way to invite God's power into your life for His greatest blessings.

Many people have been wounded in early childhood. Those wounds never heal if you avoid the hurts and pains; they only cause greater anguish and misery. Your life may never change because you try to fix things your way, and you never seek God for guidance. God created us in his image, and He wants the best for all of us. He wants to help and heal our pain and sufferings.

If you are dealing with low-self esteem because of any issues, you need to give those things back to God, so that the healing process can begin. God loves you, despite your inadequacies.

Once you begin to understand who you are as a child of God, your self-esteem will soar as high as the sky. When you pray, you will create new visions and possibilities for a changed life.

Daily Christian Prayer

Dear Heavenly Father, I Thank You for who you created me to be. I pray that if there is anything in me, unlike you, I ask that you remove daily. I also thank you for my life, and ask that you help me overcome the hurts and pains of my past. In Jesus Christ Name, Amen!

(If you are of a different faith, practice your prayer life, and faithfully communicate with God. For all women, belief in a Higher Power can bring great peace, self-acceptance, and security.)

5. Change Your Attitude

Your attitude will have a major impact on your success. IF YOU THINK NEGATIVE THOUGHTS, YOU WILL GET NEGATIVE RESULTS! Therefore, it is so important to think positively. Your mind is a powerful tool!

Sometimes we are our own worst enemy. We would like to blame our attitude on other people or situations, but the problem lies within you. You must stop criticizing yourself. When you find yourself doubting or judging yourself, replace those thoughts with encouraging, self-supportive affirmations.

Take the time to write down what you believe are the positive and negative traits that would describe you. Evaluate the list, and for each negative trait write down what you think is needed to turn it into a positive. Be realistic and only think of things that can only be changed by you. When you are finished, began to read this list on a daily basis.

Let it become embedded in your soul. Let it become your daily life guide and you will soon see the change in your attitude.

6. Surround Yourself With Positive People.

I'm sure you have heard the saying, **"What you surround yourself with is what you will become."** I believe this is true. If you have people in your life that always put you and your ideas down, your self-esteem and self-confidence may be damaged. Your life is too special to allow anyone to destroy it. You must begin to take inventory of the people around you and really evaluate the affect that they have on you. Sometimes this is a very difficult task because you may find that the individuals who are hurting you are the closest to you, such as; a mother, father, brother, sister, best friend, etc. It really doesn't matter who it is. Your life is significant, and if they truly love and respect you, they will make the effort to support you. Many times people do and say things unconsciously, and they don't know the true power of their actions. I would first suggest that you inform those that are close to you how their negative words and/or actions affect you, and give them the opportunity to correct it.

It is always healthy to associate with people who have common likes and interests. They will become your support system. You must be selective with whom you choose to share your life. Everyone may not have your best interests at hand.

As you begin to evaluate the individuals in your life, ask yourself the following questions.

- Are they a positive or negative influence?

- Do they add value, or do they devalue your life?

- Do they take advantage of your relationship with them?

- Are they chronic complainers?

- Do they fail to tell the truth?

- Do they try to control your life?

These key questions will help you make some critical changes in your life.

7. Begin to Exercise.

There are a number of benefits that come into play when you incorporate exercise into your daily routine. Exercise can lower your blood pressure, reduce stress, increase your energy, reduce tension, prevent disease, shape and tone your body, improve your blood flow, and improve endurance. The most important benefit is that it helps you feel good about yourself. It restores your self-confidence, which improves the quality of your life. Exercising is about living healthy, not about losing weight.

You should try to exercise at least 2 or 3 times a week for 30 minutes. Listen to music or read a book to help you stay focused. Make it part of your daily life and you will be satisfied with the results!

Types of Exercise

- Walking or Running (outside or on a treadmill)

- Swimming

- Dancing

- Aerobics

- Kickboxing

- Weight Training

- Cycling

- Body Building

8. Don't Give Up.

Have you ever started a project and never finished it? Or have you ever experienced some type of awkward embarrassing moment that you would like to forget? Many times we allow our past to dictate our future. We simply need to learn how to look back at certain situations and say, "So what?" We all make mistakes. When you make a mistake you should learn from it. You should probably expect to make mistakes. It's a part of life! Don't get discouraged and give up! When you find yourself wanting to give up and throw in the towel, think about all the progress you have made. Think about all the time, energy and effort you will have wasted if you give up. Don't allow yourself to become defeated. Even the most confident individuals have some insecurities. Maybe the end results are not what you expected them to be, but at least you followed through and gave it your all! Remember, nobody is perfect!

9. Treat People the Way That You Would Like to be Treated.

You might be wondering how this will help raise your self-esteem. Whatever makes you feel good will help your self-esteem. If you give compliments or do good things for other people, you will recognize the joy and happiness that your actions brought to that person, and naturally you will began to feel better. To take it a step further, think about the things that caused you to develop low self-esteem. Why would you want to inflict that pain onto someone else? You must believe that whatever you give will be given back to you. You have to be the example of what you expect from others.

For others to treat you the way that you would like to be treated, you must be the first person to change. You must teach those around you how to treat you. You have total control of what you will and will not allow. In order to accomplish this, you must know what you really want and stick with it. You must be consistent in your actions and behavior. In most circumstances, we invite the treatment that we receive, so it's up to us to change it. Start by loving and respecting yourself everyday. Don't except things that you don't like and always take a stand for what you believe in.

10. Take Action.

Last, but not least, if you really want your self-esteem to improve, you must take immediate action. You cannot expect anything to happen if you don't move forward and take control. Your life is so valuable, and its time to make a change.

Below you will find a small list of tasks that you can began instantly to give you a boost in your journey to happiness.

1. Do things that you enjoy. (i.e. dancing, skating, reading,)

2. Take good care of yourself.

3. Finish any incomplete projects.

4. Stop being self-critical.

5. Pamper yourself.

If you follow the strategies outlined in this chapter, I truly believe that your self esteem will rise. You will begin to have the self-confidence to do anything you put your mind to, and the self-respect to stand up for what you believe in.

Daily Affirmations

If you are ready to build your self-esteem, repeat these affirmations once or twice on a daily basis until they become rooted in your way of thinking.

- I am special.

- I will stand up for what I believe in.

- I love who I am.

- I am successful.

- I can do anything that I put my mind to.

- I am strong and powerful.

- I am important.

- I am smart and intelligent.

- I am a very good person.

- I am beautiful.

- I have a good attitude.

- I take pride in the things that I do.

Notes:

ABOUT THE AUTHOR

JAN FELTON

Jan Felton is President of **Attitudes** *plus*, a private consulting firm that offers training opportunities to encourage participants to experience personal fulfillment and professional success by recognizing and pursuing their potential. She is certified by Development Dimensions International and the Professional Woman Network to offer workshops to develop skills in leadership, communication, diversity, and workforce development. Jan's 35 years as an experienced educator served students in both secondary and collegiate institutions. As a former high school principal, she gained valuable skills in leadership, team building, mentoring, and communication.

The Greater Cheyenne Chamber of Commerce recognized her as the 2002 ATHENA recipient leadership in her profession and the community and for her work to help other women realize and achieve their potential.

Contact
Jan Felton, President & Consultant
Attitudes *plus*
710 West Dale Boulevard
Cheyenne, WY 82009
Phone: 307.635.2507
Fax: 307.635.2529
E-mail: j.felton@bresnan.net

TEN

THE LEADER'S IMAGE

By Jan Felton

Just as the outer wrapping of a popular chocolate candy has expanded from silver foil to include gold, purple, and striped foil (and even red and green during the holiday season), the visible image of a leader has expanded and changed, as well. We no longer think of leaders only as people in business suits or dresses who run large companies or rule countries. Our view of leaders has expanded to include those who are creative entrepreneurs, those who work from home, or stay at home with their families, and those who work in occupations that require less formal "uniforms." Leaders are often people with titles and positions; however, they can be people (co-workers or family members) who demonstrate a strong work ethic, and who lead by example because of personal power, rather than positional power. We now realize that some leaders exude confidence and charisma; some inspire by sharing their vision and setting goals; still others encourage and coach.

Although changes have occurred in the way we view the image of a leader, many of the inner qualities must endure—just like the high quality of chocolate candy in the original silver wrapper. Some additions have been made to the candies in the different-colored wrappers, additions that better suit different tastes; however, the inner strength is still the pure rich taste of the original candy. Personal power comes from within and may or may not lead to positional power (some leaders are comfortable in a support role). We need to recognize the strengths and aptitudes we possess, and value our ability to be flexible as we establish our image as a leader.

Defining the Image of a Leader.

Leaders have an inner strength that gives them a sense of personal power, and a willingness to share their gifts with others. Leaders know who they are and who they want to become; leaders help others find their strengths, identify their challenges, and empower them to grow and improve. Leaders accept challenges as gifts that offer opportunities to learn more about their ability to adapt and to achieve. Leaders recognize that life is a journey that requires them to have a variety of skills and attitudes that can be used in numerous situations that they will encounter as they travel through their personal and professional adventures. Leaders also realize their obligation to share their adventures with those with whom they live and work and to model the behaviors that will help their family members and co-workers find success and satisfaction.

As we travel on our own journey, we must learn to recognize who these leaders are, to associate with the individuals who empower us, and to develop our own leadership skills and style. For that insight, we must seek to understand what it is that sets these individuals apart, to emulate those skills and habits that are critical for leaders, and to develop our own image and style as a leader. The image we portray is the **total picture** we show to the world, as well as the **inner strength** upon which we rely as we embark on our journey. To understand the image of a leader, we must identify the characteristics and qualities we admire in others. In order to define our own image as a leader, we must recognize the qualities and characteristics we currently possess and develop those that are lacking and that are necessary to make the choices to establish ourselves as leaders, both at home and on the job. This is a journey—as exciting adventure!

What Does a Leader Look Like?

Image is a combination of an individual's outer appearance and inner strengths. When we travel, we want to choose carefully the items we pack; we need to plan and be prepared for a variety of situations. Certain standards must be met as we create an appropriate visible image; we have, however, allowed for some variety, as long as this outer appearance is representative of the type and high quality of service or product we expect. This initial impression will be based on the image presented in the first 30 seconds of an encounter. Judgment will be based on the outer wrapping, so overall appearance must represent a true picture of who you are and the message that you are confident and capable of leading and being in charge of this phase of your journey. Leaders must **look like** they are ready to lead.

Examining the "Outer Wrapping" of a Leader.

Think of a leader or leaders whom you admire; list words or phrases that describe the image that person **portrays** to the world. Think about outward appearance only for this exercise.

Leader #1:	Leader #2:
Characteristics	Characteristics
1.	1.
2.	2.
3.	3.
4.	4.
5.	5.
6.	6.

What Does a Leader Act Like?

As leaders, we must build on our inner strengths and the qualities that are characteristic of those we have admired and emulated to develop our image as a leader. We also must add those traits that make our character uniquely our own, and that allow us to adapt and grow in a variety of settings and situations. Our actions and how they are perceived by others determine our image, and true leaders must behave in a manner that instills confidence in those with whom they come in contact. Leaders must communicate with actions and words that encourage and motivate because they are always leading someone, even if only themselves. Developing and maintaining one's image is a full-time job which requires clear understanding of one's values and priorities, realistic assessment of one's skills and abilities, and true commitment to one's self and those served. Leaders must **act like** they are ready to lead.

Examining the Actions of a Leader.

Think of those same leaders that you described above. List those characteristics or actions that you consider to be descriptive of how a leader **acts** in a variety of situations.

Leader #1:	Leader #2:
Characteristics	Characteristics
1.	1.
2.	2.
3.	3.
4.	4.
5.	5.
6.	6.

What Does a Leader Sound Like?

Articulate, accurate communication is critical to enhance a leader's image and to empower those with whom she works and plays. A leader must develop skills that include proper grammar and punctuation, strong vocabulary, and appropriate tone to communicate effectively in person and in writing. A study by Dr. Albert Mehrabian at UCLA found that about 7 percent of the meaning of a message is communicated by the content (words); about 38 percent through tone and volume of voice; and about 55 percent through body language and nonverbal cues. In today's highly technical and fast-paced society, often we are establishing our image via the telephone or via e-mail, and we must be cognizant that according to the UCLA study, we have less than a 50 percent chance that our meaning will be understood as we intended it to be. Listening is a skill all leaders need to develop; both reflective and physical listening are valuable components of a leader's ability to communicate, so it is important to practice good listening habits. Appearance and tone are just as important in a written document as they are in a personal conversation. Leaders must **sound like** they are ready to lead.

Examining the Communication Style of a Leader.

Think about the manner in which the leaders you have described communicate in person or in writing. List words to describe their **communication** style; include electronic communication, as well as in-person conversation.

Leader #1:	Leader #2:
Characteristics	Characteristics
1.	1.
2.	2.
3.	3.
4.	4.
5.	5.
6.	6.

Defining Your Image as a Leader.

It is so important to remember that we are always "on display", and that our leadership skills and image are part of our daily life; we don't just lead when we are "on the job." The opportunities to lead for which we are preparing are both personal and professional; it is impossible to separate the two. When you begin to define or redefine your image as a leader, it is important to take inventory of your current persona and to assess your skills, attitudes, and habits. You must be willing to accept that, just as your life is a journey, your leadership image is a "work in progress." Recognizing who you are requires an honest look in the mirror, a realistic examination of your actions, and a sincere assessment of your ability to communicate your message. Identifying the values and priorities you consider significant will impact your ability to lead others, to manage your day-to-day duties, and to enhance your personal and professional coping strategies. When you embark on a new adventure, it is critical that you are aware of the image you present through your "outer wrapper," that you are cognizant of the messages your actions are sending, and that you need to communicate in a clear and concise manner to instill confidence in those who look to you for leadership.

Clarifying Who You Are as a Leader.

Every situation requires careful attention to the details of how you **look, act** and **sound**. For the purpose of preparing for this "leadership journey," let's consider the "outer wrapping," (persona) you share with the world, as well as the "pure rich filling" (character) that exists on the inside. How will you be perceived as a leader based on your appearance, your behaviors, and your conversations? Will this perception be a true picture of who you are? The answer to the first question will describe your persona; the answer to the second, your character. In order for you to be comfortable in your role as a leader, the two must be aligned. Think about day-to-day encounters, as well as special occasions; consider those things about you that characterize you as a confident, competent leader, regardless of your situation. Perfect practice makes perfect, so **look, act,** and **sound** like a leader, no matter what the activity; take inventory of the skills and attitudes required; select the appropriate outer wrapping; and select carefully those "inner fillings," because you are embarking on a journey that will set you apart as someone who inspires and empowers others—that's what leaders do! Just as you identified those qualities and characteristics of leaders who have inspired you, now it is time to empower yourself by defining your image—the one you have now, and the one you aspire to have as you continue on your journey to lead.

This next activity is designed to assess your authentic self—both persona and character. Complete the assessment honestly and recognize that we all have areas we consider strengths and areas we would like to improve. Once you have completed the exercise, I encourage you to give the list of words to at least two other people: one who knows you well and one who does not, but both who will be honest with you as they complete the ratings. Ask them to rate you using the same scale; do not ask them to complete the "action" column. A comparison of the ratings will give you a clear picture of how well your persona and character are aligned and of your image as a leader.

What Do I Look Like as a Leader?

Listed below are descriptors that have been generated in several workshops that I have presented on professionalism when I have asked: "What does a leader look like?" On a scale of 1 to 5 (1 = Never; 2 = Rarely; 3 = Sometimes; 4 = Often; 5 = Almost Always), please rate all of the words listed on the left as they pertain to your current appearance (outer wrapping); on the right indicate action you might take to improve any phase of your appearance that you rated 3 or below to enhance this aspect of your leader's image:

Qualities	Rating	Action
Approachable		
Appropriately dressed		
Clothing:		
Clean & wrinkle-free		
Fits body type & size		
Color coordinated		

Confident		
Jewelry (amount & style do not detract from appearance)		
Makeup natural and polished		
Makeup natural and polished		
Manicured nails		
Neat and clean		
Organized		
Pleasant (smile) and Positive		
Polished shoes		
Professional		
Up-to-date hairstyle		
Well-groomed		

Other (If you identified additional descriptors when describing the leader(s) you admire, add those words and rate them below):	

There are some excellent resources available to help you determine steps to take to improve your outward appearance. Seek professional assistance from image consultants, licensed beauticians or hair stylists; or ask a co-worker or supervisor whose image you admire for advice.

What do I act like as a leader?

Attitudes and habits are indicators of our ability to lead and to be successful in life. Listed below are descriptors workshop participants have identified as the actions of a leader. (You'll notice that some of the same words are used to describe appearance and actions.) Based on the same 5-point scale used above, rate each of these descriptors as it applies to your behaviors as a leader:

Qualities	Rating	Action
Approachable		
Coach (motivator)		
Committed (passionate)		
Compassionate		
Confident		
Courageous (risk taker)		
Confident		
Creative		
Decisive		
Dependable		
Enthusiastic		

Flexible (adaptable)		
Focused		
Goal Setter		
Good Listener		
Honest & Ethical		
Mentor (role model)		
Organized		
Problem Solver		
Punctual		
Respectful (well-mannered)		
Responsible		
Team Player		
Visionary		

Other (If you identified additional descriptors when describing the leader(s) you admire, add those words and rate them below):	

What Do I Sound Like as a Leader?

The image of a leader often is tied very closely to her ability to communicate in an effective manner with a variety of audiences. As you rate the descriptors below, consider both your verbal and written communication style. Again, use the 5-point scale to evaluate your approach to communication:

Descriptors	Rating	Action
Accurate (factual)		
Articulate		
Charismatic		
Clear		
Concise		
Courteous		
Current (up-to-date)		
Encouraging		
Enthusiastic		
Dependable		
Enthusiastic		
Good Listener		
Informed		
Knowledgeable		
Motivational		

Open		
Professional		
Respectful		
Problem Solver		
Punctual		
Respectful (well-mannered)		
Understandable		

Other (If you identified additional descriptors when describing the leader(s) you admire, add those words and rate below):	

Empowering Yourself and Others.

Now that you have assessed your image as a leader and identified those qualities you want to improve, you are ready to seek resources to provide you with the ability to enhance this aspect of your life. Observing and listening are two valuable attributes for establishing yourself as a leader and for serving as an effective mentor for others; we learn a great deal about leadership from our supervisors and co-workers.

As you continue to learn and grow, you will be ready to share your knowledge with and model behaviors for others who wish to establish themselves as leaders. Participating in professional organizations and conferences, enrolling in college classes or training workshops, reading current leadership books and magazine articles, or visiting current websites will offer you numerous methods for developing the skills and habits you deem valuable to establish your image as a leader.

Enjoy your journey, value your experiences, and invite others to join your adventure! You have many gifts to share—you are a leader!

Reading Resources

Attitude is Everything by Keith Harrell

Becoming the Professional Woman by Linda Ellis Eastman

Bringing Out the Best in Others by Thomas K. Connellan, Ph.D.

Business Etiquette for Dummies by Sue Fox

Business Etiquette: 101 Ways to Conduct Business with Charm & Savvy by Ann Marie Sabath

Customer Service & Professionalism for Women by Linda Ellis Eastman

Dress Your Best (The Complete Guide to Finding the Style That's Right for Your Body by Clinton Kelly and Stacy London

5 Steps to Professional Presence by Susan Bixler and Lisa Scherrer Dugan

How To Be Like Women of Influence by Pat and Ruth Williams

How to Say It at Work by Jack Griffin

Self-Esteem & Empowerment by Linda Ellis Eastman

The Gregg Reference Manual by William A Sabin

The Right Questions by Debbie Ford

Working with Difficult People by Muriel Solomon

You're on Stage! Image, Etiquette, Branding & Style by Linda Ellis Eastman

Notes:

_____

_____

_____

_____

_____

_____

_____

_____

_____

_____

_____

_____

_____

_____

_____

_____

_____

_____

_____

_____

ABOUT THE AUTHOR

KATHLEEN J. PENLEY, MBA

Kathleen Penley is owner of **The Penley Practice**, a management consulting firm specializing in strategic and operational planning and performance improvement. She assesses organizations to identify performance gaps, tailors solutions to align the management system, and coaches leadership in the execution of the makeover. Kathleen's work has taken her around the world, consulting, training, and providing the overall management required to ensure customer success.

Kathleen has been a key note speaker domestically and internationally. Prior to consulting, she was a senior banking executive and a corporate quality manager for a national insurance company. She has taught strategic planning and organizational behavior and development for a university MBA program.

The Department of Commerce Malcolm Baldrige National Quality Award selected Kathleen to be a Senior Examiner for five years. She is on the Executive Global Advisory Board of the Euro-American Women's Council whose mission it is to strengthen the status of women in the global marketplace. She was a member of the Board of Directors of a national credit union and a charter member of the Strategic Planning Institute Council on Benchmarking. She has an MBA and a Chartered Property Casualty Underwriter (CPCU) designation.

Contact:
Kathleen Penley
561-352-6366
kpenley@att.biz

ELEVEN

MOVING BEYOND "LIFE IS WHAT HAPPENS TO YOU!"

By Kathleen Penley

Introduction

Have you ever heard someone say, "I don't know how I got here – it just happened. I didn't plan it this way…" "I never really decided to go into insurance – I needed a job and answered an ad."

"I always meant to go back to school, but never got around to it."

I have been a consultant for twenty years and love it. Lately, however, I have been thinking about a change. Someone offered me a job, but before either of us would commit, he asked me what my goals and vision were, and where I wanted to go. I didn't have an answer! I was surprised at my stammering, since I am the one who teaches strategic planning and helps organizations and individuals to plan. But I was at a loss. I had been so busy running my business that I had forgotten to take stock of where I was and where I wanted to go.

If we don't plan, then life just happens to us. This chapter is about taking the events in your life to the next exciting level. To do this, we will discuss your vision, your strengths and weaknesses, opportunities and threats, and your strategies for achieving your vision in the next five to ten years of your life.

Many of us are examining our lives and asking ourselves, "What's next?" What do I want to do with the rest of my life? We may be on the verge of graduating from school, having children leave the nest, retiring, or have an opportunity given to us to explore new options. The question is, how will we make the most of it?

Consider all the possibilities waiting for you. Think of yourself as **"Me Unlimited"**. We never seem to give ourselves enough time to really contemplate who we are, what we want from life, and how we are going to achieve it. **We let life happen to us.** Much of our time is spent working for a company, returning home for dinner, and retiring to bed. If we spent as much time working on our own lives as we spent working for a company, our lives might be a lot richer.

So how do we do that? Read on.

What is Your Vision?

To achieve our potential, we have to know our vision – what do we want to be in three years, five years, or maybe even ten? The timeframe you choose is up to you. It's dependent on how old you are, the time it will take to achieve your vision (will it take more education or experience?), and how fast you want to achieve it. When setting the vision for "Me Unlimited", start with the phrase: "By the year 2010, I will be..." or "By 2012, I will have..."

Notice the positive words – not I *want* to be, but I ***will*** be. Always remember that the language we use is powerful.

When I really began to think of my vision, it became clear that the things I want now are intangible and harder to measure: **"I will have peace of mind, a healthy body, fun with my family and friends."** Consider hosting a "vision party" with your closest friends where you all reveal your aspirations for the next three to five years. It never hurts to have support (and accountability) available when obstacles occur to keep you from your goals and vision.

Answer this question:

By 2011, I will be... _____

_____

_____

_____

Dueling Conversations

Your mind is so powerful and often has two distinct sides "talking" to the other. There is the "I know I can do it" side, and the doubtful side, which thinks, "I will never achieve this vision." A way to overcome dueling internal conversations is to decide how you are going to keep the vision in front of you, or available for those doubtful times. You may wish to place your "vision list" in a public place, like on the refrigerator or your bedroom mirror. I tend to put mine in an envelope, which I pull out at least once a month to remind myself of who I am and what I am so eagerly pursuing. Some use a journal to help them remember and track their journey to achieving the vision. So manage that "little devil" of discouragement that wants to hold you down with positive, continuous "I will do it" affirmations.

• Where I am going to post my vision _____

Affirmations I will use:

1. _____

2. _____

3. _____

Now that we have a direction and know where we want to be, we have to determine where we are so that we can close the gap.

An environmental scan is taking a look at the world around you. If your vision is to start a new career and be financially successful, then you need to scan the marketplace to see what is available. The following questions can apply to your vision for a particular type of job, buying a house, becoming financially stable or secure, capturing a big client, and even pursuing peace of mind.

• What is the economy going to look like – are we headed for inflation or recession?

• Are there political issues existing that may interfere with your vision?

• How might upcoming elections support or hinder your vision?

- What are trends in the marketplace for employment, or for getting a big raise or bonus? How will this impact you?

If your vision is to lose weight or to enhance your image, consider other environmental issues:

- What big events are coming that might derail your vision?

- Who are your biggest supporters and detractors?

Other questions to consider include identification of your competition and what direction they are taking. You may ask what competition? It could be competition for a job! But also, have you thought about the competing forces for your time – a mother that isn't well, overtime at work, a needy friend. If our vision is to lose weight, the competition is all the chocolate cakes, pies and potato chips in our cupboards vying for our taste buds. Recognizing what is in our environment that will detract us from our vision (and more importantly those things that will support us) are keys to our success.

Take a few moments to write down the environmental barriers that are standing in the way of you achieving your vision:

1. _____

2. _____

3. _____

Next, consider those environmental forces that are pushing you to make a change:

1. _____

2. _____

3. _____

Your Strengths

Considering your vision, what are your strengths? If you are looking for a new job, what is it that you really enjoy doing – working with people, working on the computer? What do you really dislike? Are you frustrated staying in a little cubicle at work? Do you like to analyze things? Or is selling an idea your strength? What about willpower, caring for people? Are you organized, or do you do feel more comfortable with a little chaos around you? When I was doing my own strengths, I found that I really love to travel, help people, facilitate, mentor, and teach.

Strengths can be:

- **Character traits:** generous, caring, ethical, good in emergencies, tactful, energetic

- **Skills:** organizing, public speaking, selling, analyzing

- **Experience:** Leading groups of people, mentoring, facilitating diverse groups

- **Natural talents:** musical, aptitude for numbers, artistic

What are your strengths?

1. _____

2. _____

3. _____

How will these strengths help you achieve your vision?

1. _____

2. _____

3. _____

Your Weaknesses

Where are you not very strong? Be truthful! Be brave! It won't help to deceive yourself. Do you have a fear of speaking in front of people? Do you persevere when things get tough, or do you have a tendency to leave?

Ask your colleagues, friends and family what your weaknesses are, *if you dare!* You must be ready to hear things that may be difficult to accept, but unless we know where we can improve or what our blind spots are, we may do things that block the way to our vision.

List your weaknesses:

1. _____

2. _____

3.   _____

How might these weaknesses hold you back from achieving your vision?

1.   _____

2.   _____

3.   _____

Threats

What may threaten your plans? This could be demands of loved ones, changes in the workplace, such as technology that might make your position or your vision obsolete, regulations that may prevent you from performing a new service or developing a new product. Again, look to your environmental scan and personal weaknesses (or habits) for potential barriers that threaten your dream. Do you tend to self-sabotage? If your vision/dream requires a financial investment, are you a saver, or do you impulse buy and never have money in the bank? Think about it.

Obstacles that may be in the way of your vision:

1.   _____

2.   _____

3.   _____

Strategies to Move Beyond – "Life is What Happens to You."

Each of us will have different strategies, depending on what our vision is. The next step is to create a strategy or broad statement of what you are going to do, and then develop specific objective statements that support achieving that strategy and can be measured. For example, if your vision is to obtain a position in a career about which you are passionate and become recognized by your peers as an expert in the field within the next five years, your strategies and objective statements may include:

Strategy: Find a Field You Enjoy.

• Talk to people in the fields that interest you – consider your SWOT analysis.

• Find a career counselor.

• Determine the level of income you want to enjoy.

• Select your field.

Strategy: Prepare For Your Field of Endeavor.

• Determine educational requirements and enroll in school.

• Take appropriate tests, obtain necessary licenses.

• Find an internship to prepare yourself for the market.

• Utilize a life, business, or executive coach to discuss options, desires, how to develop your strengths and minimize your weaknesses.

Strategy: Expand Your Network of Contacts.

• Identify networking groups associated with your field of interest.

• Join an "affinity group" that has similar interests as you.

• Select a mentor to guide you and introduce you to influential people.

Strategy: Select a Company/Career That Meets Your Needs.

• Identify the company you want to pursue, or start your own.

• Locate contacts that can help you from your networking.

Strategy: Live Your Passion!

• Determine what it will take to become the best, and how you will determine you have reached that pinnacle.

• Expand your networking reach.

• Become a public speaker about your passion.

• Write a chapter in a book!

In any of these endeavors, it will be most helpful to have the support of a coach and/or mentor to challenge you with difficult but necessary questions, to act as a sounding board, to keep you from sabotaging yourself when the little devil on your shoulder gets in the way.

Don't Let Life Just Happen to You.

Live life so that when you reach your final day on earth, you can say, "I did it – I reached my goal!" May you have clarity and determination to follow your passion and pursue your vision. It is attainable.

ABOUT THE AUTHOR

DR. BRENDA WARD

Brenda E. Ward, Ph.D., DSE, is Founder and President of Bren-Barr Associates, Inc., a Professional and Personal Development Education and Training Consulting Company, located in Long Island, New York. Her extensive professional experience spans twenty-five years. She is an accomplished education and training specialist, corporate executive, motivational leader and mentor. She provides distinctive education and training services on a range of topics to individuals and the general workforce in various corporate environments nationally.

Prior to starting her company, she enjoyed a most progressive and rewarding career as a Registered Professional Nurse, and held senior executive positions in major teaching hospitals in the New York Metropolitan area; the latest as Vice President of Nursing Services and Education.

Dr. Ward is an active member of The Professional Woman Network International Speakers Bureau, involved in speaking and teaching internationally, is an appointed Distinguish Special Envoy to the United Nations University and Social and Economic Council and a member of various other professional organizations including, The International Third World Leaders Association. She is also active in voluntary community service in Nassau County, New York, has written articles in various professional publications and is a co- author of the book, Becoming The Professional Woman.

Her academic credentials include, a Ph.D. in Health and Human Services, Post Masters Certificate in Nursing Administration, Master of Arts in Community Health Education, Bachelor of Arts in Health Sciences, New York State Registered Professional Nurse License and certification as Diversity Educator and Youth Relations Trainer.

Dr. Ward is the recipient of the 2005 Healthcare Professional of the Year Award from the Concerned Sisters Club of New York, the 2001 Dynamic Woman of The Year Award from Assemblyman Perry of Brooklyn, New York; The Outstanding Community Service and Dedication to the Nursing Profession Award from New York Counties Registered Nurses Association District 13; The Outstanding Contribution to Human Services Award from Chi Eta Phi Sorority, Inc. of Nassau County, New York, and Outstanding Community Service Award from the Nassau County Legislature and the County Executive.

Contact
Brenda E. Ward, Ph.D., DSE
Bren-Barr Associates, Inc.
3280 Sunrise Highway, # 398,
Wantagh, NY 11793
Tel: (516) 221-6989
Email:Brenbarr@optonline.net
www.Brenbarr.com

TWELVE

FROM GOOD TO EXCELLENT CUSTOMER SERVICE

By Dr. Brenda Ward

The power of positive customer relationships in the workplace cannot be underestimated or ignored. Savvy, successful leaders have recognized this fact and have taken giant steps to maintain their growth and competitive edge.

Is the Customer Always Right?

The well known saying, "the customer is always right," is often taken literally, but should not be. Let us explore this. Bear in mind that each one of us is a customer.

1. Can we honestly say that in our capacity as a customer we are
    always right? I would venture to say that, most of us would agree
    that we are not.

2. What then, is the true meaning of this saying? To my mind, the
    true meaning is, "always treat the customer right." This basically
    means treat the customer in the right manner; the way you would
    like to be treated and would like your family and loved ones to
    be treated.

A clear understanding of the difference between customer service,
customer satisfaction and customer relations is an important first step
in any process to accomplish moving customer service from good
to excellent.

- **What Is Customer Service?**

  In the simplest and most expansive term, it is whatever is
  done to meet the needs and expectations of a customer.

- **What Is Customer Satisfaction?**

  It is the difference between how a customer expects to be
  treated and how he or she perceives being treated.

- **What Is Customer Relations?**

  It is the interaction with customers – the relationship that
  exists between the service provider and the customer. It is
  within this realm that customer expectations fall.

- **What Is Excellent Customer Service**

  It is providing service that competently meets the customer's specific needs and exceeds the customer's expectations; resulting in an increased level of customer satisfaction, loyalty and customer relations.

One imperative is to understand that the quality of customer service determines the level of customer satisfaction. The desire for excellent customer satisfaction therefore, is the engine that drives customer service from good to excellent. Remember that customers may be satisfied with the performance of a task that met their specific need, yet may have some degree of dissatisfaction with the overall service experience. Most often this is because their general expectations were not met to their satisfaction.

THE PATHWAY TO EXCELLENT CUSTOMER SERVICE.

<pre>
                          Excellent
        ⇒⇒⇒⇒ ⇒   Customer   ⇒⇒⇒⇒ ⇒
             ⇑   Relations   ⇓
             ⇑   ⇓   ⇓
Needs & Expectations   ⇒ Excellent   ⇐ Excellent Customer
Met at High Level   Customer Service   Satisfaction
             ⇑   ⇓
             ⇑   ⇑   ⇓
        ⇐ ⇐ ⇐ ⇐ High workforce ⇐ ⇐ ⇐
                        satisfaction
</pre>

A frequently asked question is, am I supposed to know the expectations of all the customers? The answer is a resounding yes, because each one of us is a customer, and we know what our general expectations are. Ours are no different from those whom we serve.

Let's take a few moments to do the following activity together.

Activity

Assume that you are a customer in a bank. List some of the general expectations that you have of your service provider, aside from skill. (What type of interaction do you expect from the bank employees?)

Location: Bank
Expectations of employees:

1. _____

2. _____

3. _____

4. _____

5. _____

Expectations

Most customers have basic expectations. Match the answers you gave from your "bank" experience with the following:

- To be acknowledged

- To be treated with dignity and respect

- To receive prompt, courteous service

- The privacy of my transaction and all other information to be maintained

- To be provided with timely, accurate information in an understandable manner

- To be treated pleasantly and professionally

These are just a few of the general expectations of a relationship nature that all customers have. They are reasonable and achievable.

What behaviors of the bank employees would have exceeded your expectations?

Customer Expectations Exceeded by:

*   _____

*   _____

*   _____

*   _____

*   _____

Now ask yourself the following questions:

- Are these expectations reasonable and achievable?

    Yes_____   No_____

- Would I do business with an establishment if these expectations were not being met?

  Yes_____   No_____

It is vital to constantly monitor customer satisfaction within any business.

- The customer best evaluates the quality of service.

- Service evaluation should begin at point of contact between customer and employee.

- A customer service evaluation should be ongoing.

- The customer evaluation tool should be specific, and clearly determine the degree to which the customer was (or was not) satisfied.

Example

On a scale of 1 to 5, with 5 being the highest level, indicate how well your expectations were met during this banking experience.					
Timeliness of service	1	2	3	4	5
Courtesy	1	2	3	4	5
Maintenance of privacy	1	2	3	4	5

Factors Affecting Customer Relations

It is to be acknowledged that there are factors that can adversely affect the quality of customer relations and satisfaction in any work environment. These include, but are not limited to:

• **The Quality of the Infrastructure**

This refers to how effective and efficient the operating systems, equipment, procedures, and policies that support the services are. Remember that the maintenance of the infrastructure is everyone's responsibility. It is the responsibility of the management to insure that the infrastructure is solidly in place, but it is those who utilize the various components of the infrastructure who are accountable to maintain its integrity.

Example: The individual who breaks a piece of equipment is responsible for initiating the replacement of repair process. This may be as simple as reporting the break to the appropriate source/person, or removing the equipment from circulation.

Let me take a moment to share with you an incident that has positively and profoundly impacted me to be consistently vigilant and supportive of my infrastructure during my many successful years as a leader.

While in elementary school in Jamaica, West Indies, sewing was a part of the Home Economics Curriculum for all girls. Each Friday afternoon, the girls would go to their sewing class and the boys to their woodwork or some other technical work class. Each girl was required to bring their own needle to the sewing class. Well, I did not like to sew (for the record, I still do not). The teacher decided that I should make an apron. I independently decided that I would not sew the apron because I did not need one. As a result, I would go to the sewing class each Friday without a needle, but would be sure to have a straight pin. I would tie a piece of thread around the head of the straight pin, and each time the teacher came around to check to see if I was sewing, I would plunge the pin into the fabric as though I was sewing.

*After a few weeks, she came and took the fabric to see how close I was to completing the project. To her amazement, she discovered that there was not one stitch on the material. She became very angry, and of course gave me the dreaded punishment. After school dismissal, I was to write two hundred times, the following: "**No workman can work without his tools, and no little girl can sew without a needle.**" The problem was compounded for me because I knew that this was not the only punishment I would get for the one infraction. I was already experiencing mentally the one I would get from my mother when I got home. Needless to say, I learned my lesson.*

The point I wish to drive home here is the content of the lines I had to write about working without the tools. Remember, as leaders we cannot expect the workforce to work without the necessary tools, equipment, policies, procedures, training, and support. The infrastructure must be solid and functional.

• The Quality of Staff Encounters

This is the customer relation aspect, where attitude, behavior and cultural sensitivity are the main focus. Michael LeBouf, in *"How To Win Customers and Keep Them For Life"*, states that 68% of customers stop doing business with service providers because of an attitude of indifference toward the customer by employees.

Sensitivity and responsiveness to diversity is a critical aspect to be addressed in any process to move customer service from good to excellent. Bearing in mind that diversity has various dimensions, including but not limited to ethnic identity, age, gender, sexual preference, religion, and the physically and mentally challenged, it is incumbent upon leaders to insure that the workforce is appropriately sensitized to relate effectively to diverse customer groups. Stereotyping in the workplace must be avoided at all cost.

Leaders must lead by precept and example. When there is visible evidence that leaders embrace diversity, they serve as catalysts for creating and maintaining a workforce that is sensitive to diversity. Remember, the workforce looks for evidence of commitment from their leaders, so the leader must take seriously the common saying, "**If you talk the talk, you must walk the walk.**"

Communicating With Customers

When communicating with customers, there should be a heightened sense of awareness of the role of the staff as ambassadors representing their establishment, organization or business, as well as themselves. Therefore, their communication should be in a manner that reflects the highest standards, values and self-control.

Attitude and behavior are both modes of communication that are extremely powerful.

Because emotion or feelings are the trigger for attitude and behavior, which includes self-control, there must be keen sensitivity to the importance of controlling our responses during interactions with customers. Responses communicate volumes about not only the individuals' self-control but also the work environment. Recognize that there are two main types of responses:

1. Reactive Response: Emotionally-driven; lack of self-control; defensive

2. Responsive Response: Calm; Positive attitude; professional behavior

Responding rather than reacting is the attitude and behavior of choice when relating to customers.

Activity

As customers, we have all had good and bad experiences. Think about one of the **worst** customer service experiences you have had. Identify and briefly state what the problems were that led to your dissatisfaction. (i.e. attitude, behavior, competence, unsatisfactory environment, lack of attention). Was an employee "reactive" rather than responsive?

Poor Customer Service Experience

Where was it?
What happened?
What, if anything, did you do about the experience?
Do you continue to do business with the service provider?
Do you continue to do business with the service provider?
How many people did you tell about your experience, and why?
List your most positive customer service experience: Store/company name: Positive experience:

Leaders must be open and receptive to feedback from customers and the workforce, regardless of whether the feedback is positive of not. Whenever necessary, prompt and effective corrective measures must be implemented to insure mutually satisfying outcomes. Every effort must be made to share compliments with the workforce. This is a powerful source of motivation for them to maintain and improve customer service. (Correct poor behavior in private, and praise in public.) Provide ongoing customer evaluations, which are provided to clients and in easy viewing/access. Hold meetings with employees to discuss problem areas and also excellent service. Consider providing recognition awards for those employees providing **excellent** (not just "good") customer service.

Some Key Principles for Service Excellence

Steps for the Leader and employees to follow:

- Behave and perform as if you own the business, and make excellent service your mantra.

- Be aware that customer service begins at the first contact with the customer, both verbal and non-verbal, by telephone, or face-to-face.

- Always acknowledge the customer and have the staff introduce themselves in a friendly, sincere manner.

- Call the customer by name. Never use the customer's first name unless given permission to do so.

- Identify and respond effectively to meet customer expectations. Encourage employees to ask, "How may I help you?" at the first encounter, and "Is there anything else I can do for you?" at the end of each encounter.

- Embrace diversity sensitively, remembering that all people have the same general expectations, and must be recognized and accepted as individuals rather than be stereotyped.

- Take responsibility for the quality of service that is provided.

- Integrate the principles of concern, good communication, positive customer relations, and competence into routine service practices.

- Be polite. Politeness is to do and say the kindest things in the kindest ways. Remember to say, "Please," "May I?", etc.

- Be respectful and use good manners.

- Be friendly and helpful without being familiar or overbearing.

- Remember the importance of non-verbal communication, and to be responsive rather than reactive.

- Make an effort to educate the customer about the services provided. Sy Syms, owner of a retail store in New York, says, "An educated consumer is our best customer." He has a very successful business.

- Look at the customer as they listen and talk. This helps to build rapport and establish a trusting relationship.

- Maintain a pleasant expression.

- Acknowledge and be prepared to apologize for any fracture in service.

- Always make an effort to correct any problem and/or compensate for the problem – This is called "**service recovery**." Seek help, make referrals, or offer alternatives whenever possible. When appropriate, ask the customer to participate in the problem-solving process by suggesting corrective measures. This indicates a willingness to cooperate, resolve the problem amicably, and be partners with the customers.

- Do your best to have the customer leave satisfied, because the success and security of the establishment, organization, business depends upon the customer.

It is clear that elevating customer service from good to excellent is a challenge that is beyond the ability of any single individual to accomplish unilaterally. It essentially demands the efforts of a committed team that understands and appreciates the vast array of interplaying variables that impact such a course of action. The crucial responsibility of the leader in an endeavor such as this is to establish trust, and maintain an open line of communication with the workforce. This facilitates trust and cooperation, which are vital sources of motivation. These together form the foundation of a healthy, progressive and successful work environment, and are also key ingredients in the recipe for personal and professional success at all levels. And remember, if each employee feels a sense of ownership within the company, they will go the extra step to customer service excellence.

As a leader, do everything possible to have every employee feeling that they are an integral part of the team.

Notes:

ABOUT THE AUTHOR

NOTHRICE ALFORD

Nothrice Alford, ED. S. received her undergraduate degree in Elementary Education from Albany State University, her Master Degree from Georgia State University and her Education Specialist Degree from Troy State University. She was certified as a Reading Recovery Teacher at Georgia State University. She is listed in the 2006 edition of Who's Who Among American Teachers. She recently retired after 30 years of teaching in Georgia. She was recently named to Cambridge Who's Who.

Ms. Alford is the CEO and President of The Heritage Institute for Personal Excellence, a coaching and training consulting organization. She is a member of The Professional Woman Network (PWN).

She is a contributing author in, A Train Runs Through It, a book of stories and memories about her hometown. She is also a contributing author for Survival Skills for the African-American Woman and the forthcoming book Women as Leaders: Strategies for Empowerment & Communication.

Nothrice Alford is available for presentations, seminars, workshops, consultation, and coaching on a regional, national, and international basis.

Contact
The Heritage Institute of Personal Excellence
P.O. Box 40
Mableton, GA 30126
nothrice@bellsouth.net
www.protrain.net

THIRTEEN

SELF-EMPOWERMENT: DISCOVERING THE POWER WITHIN

By Nothrice Alford

There is a power within you that is stronger than any other power. Inside each of us are **dreams and desires**. Self-empowerment is the key to reaching your goals and desires in life. In it's simplest form, self-empowerment means taking charge of your own life. Self-empowered individuals do not give their power away; they vigorously hold onto it, even when challenged.

Self-empowerment is key to creating your own future. It means that you are taking control of your approach to life, your habits, your choices, and overall directions. You have within you the power to create a different future, to choose how you want to live and who you want to be. Grant yourself the power to assume responsibility for your own life.

There is a powerful Spirit inside of each one of us, and it is that Spirit that gives you such power that whatever you become aware of is what you will have in your life—by virtue of your own consciousness (awareness). You have within you talents, intelligence and creativity that can only come out when you make a demand on it. You must make a demand on the power within you. If you do not make a demand on it, you will never know what is possible.

All that we are and all that we hope to be are the results of the power within each of us. It will take true commitment to evolve into the empowerment of one's self. The number seven represents completion. Follow these seven steps to self-empowerment.

Step One: Awareness

The first step is to **reconstruct your thoughts**. Self-empowerment is mastering your ability to take control of your thoughts. Your inner thoughts create your outer world. Think positive thoughts. Do not entertain thoughts that do not empower you toward your goals and desires. Dwell only on those activities and events that you want to occur in your life. Your power to think is unlimited. Think thoughts and do things that will allow you to live the life you want to live here and now. It is what you do daily that creates the circumstances of your life.

Come into the awareness that nothing is impossible and that all things are possible. Think big! Donald Trump once said in an interview, "I knew I was going to think, so I might as well think big!"

Your thoughts have power. We have more than 50,000 thoughts a day. Thinking is the only activity that the spirit processes. So be very careful of what you are thinking. Keep changing your thoughts until the old thinking does not enter your mind at all anymore. Your awareness will draw unto you whatever it is that you are most aware of.

Entertain and observe thoughts that empower you. What you repeatedly hear and see, you become. When thoughts of lack occur, replace them with thoughts of plenty. When thoughts of negativity occur, replace them with thoughts of positivity. Turn your obstacles into opportunities by looking beyond the appearance that seems limited. Do not become a victim of the thoughts others are giving you. Speak immediately the thoughts that you wish to be your reality. Do you have limiting beliefs? If so, what are your limiting beliefs?

Step Two: Meditation

Meditation is a safe, gentle and effective method to lower blood pressure, reduce stress, increase mental clarity, and improve the overall quality of life. Find a place or create a space in your home to meditate. This is where you will do your prayer work, your reading and meditating. That place will become powerful because you go there to do your meditation work. Meditation is a key component of prayer.

The purpose of meditation is to expand your awareness of the power within. Take time each day to seek the power within through prayer and meditation. Align with the power within and you will discover your purpose, your desires, and your goals for life. In silence, still any anxious thoughts so that you may hear the guidance from within.

It is through meditation that you will be empowered to accomplish your goals and desires. Connect everyday to your higher power.

Meditation involves turning your attention inward to the mind itself and shutting out the outer world appearance. When you mediate, listen for directions. Listen to your inner voice. Your desires and passion will often come as a whisper that reminds you of what is important and makes you happy.

Step Three: Clarity of Purpose

Clarity is power. Everything you are going through has a purpose. We are often presented with many choices in life. Sometimes we are unsure of what to do and what decision we should make. That is when you should go within to seek understanding and clarity. Listen to your heart. Trust the power within you to bring forth the clarity you need to make the right choice.

You will reach a level of clarity regarding the situations in your life when you gain personal awareness. This is achieved by tuning in to your self more clearly during mediation. Ask yourself, what is it that I really want? Do you really want what you are asking for, or is it someone else's idea of what you should be doing. It is easy to give up when you are not clear and specific about your vision. Be specific about your desires. Be clear. You have to be clear because if you are not clear about what you want in life, you will not obtain your goals or desires. What is it you really desire?

Step Four: Commitment

Once you are clear about your desire, commit to achieving it. Commit to believing in you. You need to be driven by your goals and desires that matters most to you. Just because something is a challenge does not mean it was not meant to be. Never give up. Do the things you really want to do, even though something else would be easier. Don't quit. Make a decision to persevere until your goal is achieved.

The power of repetition is key to reprogramming your habits. It is your belief system that has to change. It is what is deep inside of you. The way to change your belief is by replacing the old with the new through repetition. Do the same thing every day toward reaching your goal. What you repeatedly do will ultimately become an integral part of you. As you develop your new pattern, you will be able to do more, but first make it a habit.

Be determined. It is up to you to give the orders to your subconscious mind, and it is up to you to stand firm in a decisive way. Until you make the decision, you will just wander through life not knowing which way to go or what to do. Once you make the decision, never give up. Giving up is not an option. The key to good decision-making is listening to the voice within for guidance and then acting on it. Spend time each day working on your decision.

Commit to things that empower you. Go beyond your comfort zone. Go the distance. Be enthusiastic. Enthusiasm means having a positive mental attitude. Enthusiasm will inspire you to move forward with your desires and goals. Keep your commitment and take small steps to make it happen. You must be consistent. Whatever you give your attention to, you will create more of the same.

What are you committed to?

Step Five: Have a Plan

Preparation is key to your success. The simplest and most effective technique for achieving any goal is to write it down. Read your goals each day and think about the process involved in reaching your goals.

Post your plan where you will see it frequently. Put it on your refrigerator or your bathroom mirror.

Write Down Your Three Top Goals or Desires.

1. _____

2. _____

3. _____

Take specific steps and strategies to achieve your goals. Achieving your vision may not happen in the time frame you would prefer, but if you plan your work and work your plan, you will triumph. Know why you want what you want. Be sure what you want is aligned with what matters most to you. What action would move you closer to your true goal right now?

Step Six: Be Prepared

Take the first step in making your goal a reality. Develop the skills you need to be successful. Continue to educate and train yourself. Take classes in areas you are interested in most. Read books that are related to your desires and goals. Reading sharpens the mind. Associate with people who are doing the things you want to do in life. Be with people who support you and your goals. Associate with people who are successful. Ninety percent of the results we get come from the people we associate with.

Join organizations that are affiliated with your goals and desires.

You must be prepared to learn as you go along. You must discover how to learn again and continue to do so. You will grow as a person and will handle situations more effectively. You have to be prepared mentally as well as physically to be empowered. Make sure you are doing your part to be prepared. Invest in yourself by taking the following steps below.

Steps For a Healthy Body and Mind.

1. **Proper nutrition**—eat healthy snacks and meals.

2. **Body maintenance**—maintain proper weight for your height.

3. **Appropriate exercise**—exercise at least three days a week

4. **Appropriate sleep**—get eight hours of sleep each night.

5. **Respect your body**—take care of your body.

There is nothing that can come into your day that you will not be prepared to handle when you are aligned with the power within you. Discern what is important in life and give priority to it. Act with courage and confidence. Move forward while making the best use of your time and resources. It is what you do daily that creates the circumstances of your life. Take a leap of faith and trust in your gut feeling. What steps will you take to achieve your goals and desires?

Step Seven: Take Action

"Take Action" means to do, to act, to move, to put into place. When you gain knowledge, you have to apply it. By following these seven steps, you can achieve your goals and desires. Awareness has two parts. They are knowledge and action. It takes courage to take action.

Take action now to achieve your goals and desires. What makes us different is not what we know, but what we do. It is only through our actions that we create different results. You must have the will to take action. You must also be able to step out of your "comfort zone."

Your success is just on the other side of your comfort zone. Go beyond your comfort zone. Be willing to be uncomfortable in a new situation. What steps are you going to take to gain your power? What actions are you going to take toward self-empowerment?

List 5 Things You Are Going to Start Next Week Toward Self-Empowerment:

1. _____

2. _____

3. _____

4. _____

5. _____

Commit to three hours per week in developing yourself. Write a mission statement for yourself. Post it in a visible place where you can see it and read it each day. Your mission statement will help to stay focus on what matters to you the most. Remember, it is only by your actions that you determine your results.

What Is Next For You?

You have within you the potential, abilities and talents to do what has to be done. It is what is deep inside of you that has to change. Absolutely nothing will change in your life unless you make a conscious choice to do something different. As you accept responsibility for your life, you will be empowered to create it according to your desires. Be true to yourself. When you choose your action, you will create the consequences. Believe in yourself! If you believe you can, you will succeed. Claim your power now!

ABOUT THE AUTHOR

CHLOE D. MERRILL, PH.D., CFCS, CFLE

Dr. Chloe D. Merrill is the owner of Transformational Symmetry Consulting, LLC, which is a team of specialists trained in personal and corporate effectiveness. Founded in 1996 to inspire, motivate and guide individuals and organizations through "Continuous Change with Balance", Transformational Symmetry Consulting, LLC, links together the mind, body, and spirit to help improve productivity, creativity, memory, energy, ability to communicate with yourself and others, and overall improve quality of life.

Chloe is a Professor at Weber State University, Moyes College of Education, Department of Child and Family Studies. Chloe served as Department Chair from 1987 to 1995. She is certified in Family and Consumer Sciences (CFCS), a Certified Family Life Educator (CFLE), as well as certified to teach Secondary and Early Childhood Education.

Chloe is a member and active in numerous professional organizations. She is affiliated with civic and educational associations where she has or is currently serving as a board and committee member. Some include: Professional Woman Network, an international consulting organization; National Association of Female Executives; National Council on Family Relations; and the American Association of Family and Consumer Sciences. As a motivational speaker, conference and workshop lecturer, Chloe strives to educate all participants with knowledge that will help them throughout their lives.

Chloe has received numerous awards. Some include: Meritorious Service Award, National Council on Family Relations, 2001; Special Recognition award for Outstanding Service to the AAFCS Business Section, American Association of Family and Consumer Sciences, 1999; Outstanding Service to the Certified Family Life Educator Program Award, National Council on Family Relations, 1998; Lowe Innovative Teaching Award, Weber State University, 1998; Leader Award, American Association of Family and Consumer Sciences, 1998; Leader Award, Utah Association of Family and Consumer Sciences, 1997; and the Endowed Scholar for the College of Education, Weber State University from 1993-1997.

Chloe is a co-author in the books *Self-Esteem and Empowerment for Women, You're on Stage! Image, Etiquette, Branding & Style.* and *Women's Journey to Wellness: Mind, Body, & Spirit* published by the Professional Woman Publishing. Chloe's next book is entitled *Women as Leaders: Strategies for Empowerment & Communication.*

Chloe was born in Carbon County, Utah. She graduated with an Associates Degree from College of Eastern Utah, Bachelors and Master Degree from Utah State University, and Doctorate from Colorado State University. She and/or her team of specialists are available for presentations on a local, national, and international basis.

Contact
Transformational Symmetry Consulting, LLC
P.O. Box 150064
Ogden, UT 84415
Phone/Fax: 801-392-7465
http://transformationalsymmetry.com
E-mail: Transformationalsymmetry@comcast.net

FOURTEEN

YOU THE LEADER: BUILDING BETTER RELATIONSHIPS

By Chloe D. Merrill

Everyone has an opportunity to be a leader at some time in their life. How effective a person is with a leadership opportunity depends on many variables. Effective leaders know how to create positive relationships with those they lead, so that they will be more effective leaders. Our society today presents many opportunities to be a leader. Opportunities include being a leader in their family, at work, during relaxation and play, during worship time, volunteer activities, or when they are learning. The most effective leaders know they cannot do it alone and must create and cultivate positive relationships in order for their group to achieve its goal.

It does not matter if the goal is to play a game, study for a test, clean the house, or complete a multi-million dollar project. Positive relationships make the task more enjoyable, while also making each member of the group feel valued and needed. Being part of a team that cannot get along, has a leader who says my way or the highway, who is incapable of creating the team atmosphere, or does not let the members know they are needed and valued can be frustrating and demoralizing. A leader cannot lead alone; they must have one or more people working with them to be called a leader. A group will function much more efficiently if the leader creates a team atmosphere where members feel valued and needed. When a person feels valued and needed, they will go above and beyond what they are asked to do. Creating positive relationships is the effective leader's secret weapon. Those positive relationships will have ripples in all areas of a person's life.

Life presents each person with many opportunities to choose to be a leader or a follower. Regardless of whether choosing to be a leader or a follower, creating and cultivating positive relationships will enhance the experience. Developing and maintaining relationships is a life-long commitment. Whatever their age or experience, a person's relationships will present them with new and demanding challenges. Often times we lead by the example we set for others.

People and Change

All people change over time. While change in children is visible and obvious, change for adults is gradual, but it is still there. As people change, relationships change for better or worse. Many times change in life is expected and people have "milestones and hurdles." Other times unexpected change can present challenges or threats to the relationship.

A leader helps people move through these different times in life to see what changes might need to be made. These changes could be in your family, at work, in the community you live in, or with others that seek you out as a role model.

People often get emotional, hurt, or even angry when others have different values, beliefs or expectations than they do. There needs to be an understanding and acceptance developed between two or more people that helps them understand that differences in ideas and expectations, and even conflict and strong expression of feelings will be part of the relationship. A leader can make or break a group, no matter how it is defined. The attitudes and behavior of the leader strongly influence the group's performance, and also the amount of satisfaction each individual group member will receive. Effective leaders know that, if they create and cultivate relationships with those who are assigned or choose to follow them, they are on the path to leadership and interpersonal success.

You, The Leader Model

Following is a model to help you become a leader and have better relationships with those you lead, no matter what the situation.

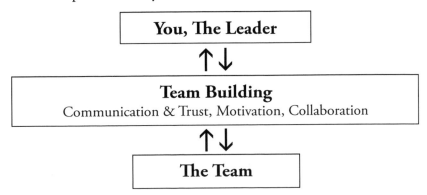

You, The Leader

Often, you hear that statement, "They are a born leader." This is what many people thought until researchers made leadership a legitimate subject for intense investigation. What was found was that leadership was much more complex than being born with the right genes. It is also more than the ability to give directions to the followers.

Being a leader of a group does not make a person one. It is necessary that the leader have the knowledge and tools to earn the acceptance of the group members, if the leader is to have an influence on the group's behavior. When being a leader turns out to be a bad experience, it is almost always because of the leader's own ineffectiveness. Few people get any kind of specific training in leader effectiveness.

In order to be a successful leader, a person must be willing and able to recognize their own strengths and weaknesses. They also need to be able to identify a problem within their team and see that it gets solved. People, even leaders, do not always have an easy time changing because old habits die hard, but an effective leader has to take the lead in implementing those changes, starting with themselves.

Exercise

Following is a list of some leadership qualities.

1. Circle the qualities that you feel you have at this time.

2. Have a family member, friend, colleague, or someone that knows you well circle the qualities that they feel you have.

Compare the two lists. If you question a quality that the other person has circled, talk to them about why they feel you have this quality.

LEADERSHIP QUALITIES

Honest	Goal oriented	Humble	Committed
Optimistic	Thoughtful	Resilient	Creative
Prompt	Cheerful	Competent	Dependable
Friendly	Expressive	Flexible	Forgiving
Healthy	Enthusiastic	Motivated	Hard-working
Sense of humor	High integrity	Fun loving	Persistent
Non-judging	Sensitive	Passionate	Organized
Spontaneous	Energetic	Compassionate	Good listener
Intelligent	Positive thinker	Assertive	Consistent
Personable	Non-blamin	Responsible	Loyal

Team Building

From the very first meeting of the team, it is the responsibility of the leader to create positive communication that will allow the team to function at it its best. Taking the time to get to know the members of the team, and what is important to them, sets the team up for success. Whether the team is comprised of family members, friends or colleagues, finding out what is important to the relationship or task will help the leader be more effective. Many times leaders are so focused on what needs to be accomplished they forget to cultivate the relationships that will make the task easier.

Creating and cultivating the relationships within the group is a way to meet the team member's needs. Maslow created a hierarchy of needs that helps to explain why humans behave the way they do in certain situations. The pyramid starts at the bottom and works its way up. If a person does not have their physiological and safety needs met, they will have a hard time focusing on anything else. If those needs are met, then it is possible to move up to the next level.

MASLOW'S HIERARCHY OF NEEDS

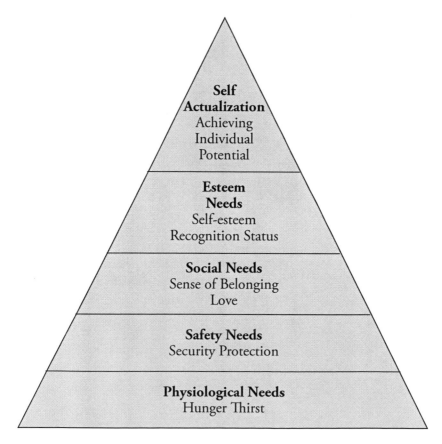

The next two levels from Maslow's hierarchy of needs fit especially well into team building, Belonging and Esteem. Belonging needs introduce our tribal nature: If you are helpful and kind to others, they will want you as friends. Esteem needs are for higher power in a group: If people respect you, you have greater power. An effective leader is a person who has the skills to meet the needs of the people involved in the group or organization and the leader themselves. Unless the leader is relatively free from the pressure of their own needs, they will not be in a mood to help others.

Creating relationships is one means to satisfying these needs, as the group identifies assesses and clarifies problems and issues to be resolved. Team building is the process of enabling a group of people to reach their goal or goals. The primary skill in the team building process is recognizing the right issues, and tackling them in an appropriate way and an appropriate order. Team building can also take a different form, depending on the size and nature of the group.

Some steps in team building are:

- Choose your team carefully. Sometimes your team will already be chosen for you; an example would be your family.

- Listen to suggestions, ideas, criticisms, and complaints. Act on these and let people know what you have done.

- Recognize/reward individuals and the "team" for achievements.

- Involve key people in planning, decisions and changes.

- Keep members informed of plans, decisions, and changes.

- Show members that their work is important to the team's success.

- Show you trust team members to complete tasks.

Exercise

Imagine you are going to be leading a new book club or other group. You chose three of the members and they recommended three other members, whom you do not know. Since you started the club or group, you chose the first book and the first meeting will be in your home. You will have to explain how the club will work and what will be expected of each member. Before you can jump into the discussion, you must create a focus that meets the needs of the club or group and the members. Come up with 5-6 questions that can be used to get to know each other and what the members are hoping to get from the club or group. (If you cannot connect to the book club idea, think of another club you would like to be in, i.e., gardening club, art appreciation, backpacking or another group such as at your work or in your neighborhood.)

1. _____
   _____
   _____
   _____
   _____

2. _____
   _____
   _____
   _____
   _____

3. _____
   _____

_____

_____

_____

4. _____

_____

_____

_____

_____

5. _____

_____

_____

_____

_____

6. _____

_____

_____

_____

_____

Communication and Trust

Communication is an essential skill in a good relationship of any type. Good communication does not come naturally, however. Some people are better communicators than others. It is the leader's responsibility to help the team set the ground rules for acceptable positive communication. The leader also needs to make sure to model positive communication at all times. Communication is not just talking. A great deal of information is sent without using words; your body posture, the tone of your voice, and the expression on your face can change the meaning of your message. These non-verbal means of communicating can tell the group how you feel about them. If your feelings do not fit with the words, it tends to be the non-verbal communication that gets heard and believed.

Communication can be improved by learning and practicing some simple skills:

- Use "I" statements when talking to others about your thoughts or feelings. This promotes ownership of what you are saying, which establishes a strong position.

- Ask for what you need/want. Limit your expectations that other people should know what you want. The best chance of receiving what you want is to speak up and ask for it!

- Check out assumptions. Misunderstandings can arise from acting on what you guess people in your group want. Do not make assumptions.

- Resolve conflicts. Be sure to negotiate and compromise. Start the problem solving by listening to and respecting each other's point of view. Conflicts are more easily addressed when the people participate in the solution, instead of one person dominating the decision making process. Aim for a balance.

Be a good listener:

- Keep comfortable eye contact.

- Lean towards the person speaking and make appropriate gestures to indicate interest and concern.

- Have an "open" position – fairly relaxed posture, with arms and legs uncrossed.

- Face people – do not sit or stand sideways.

- Realize that physical barriers, such as noise or interruptions, are likely to make effective communication difficult.

Trust is a key element in creating a team and building relationships. As a leader, how do you create an environment of trust? It starts with you. First you need to honestly say that you trust yourself. Ralph Waldo Emerson stated, "Who you are speaks so loudly I cannot hear what you say." Learn to trust yourself and that translates to how others treat you.

Trust in other people can be grounded in your evaluation of a person's ability, integrity, and kindness. The more you observe these characteristics in another person, the more your level of trust in that person is likely to grow. Ability refers to an assessment of the other's knowledge, skill, or competency. This recognizes that trust requires some sense that the other is able to perform in a manner that meets your expectations.

Integrity is the degree to which the person adheres to principles that are acceptable to you. This leads to trust based on consistency of past actions, credibility of communication, commitment to standards of fairness, and the congruence of the other's word and deed.

Kindness is your assessment that the trusted individual is concerned enough about your welfare to either advance your interests, or at least not impede them. The other's perceived intentions or motives of the person are most central. Honest and open communication, delegating decisions, and sharing control indicate evidence of one's benevolence.

Motivation

Creating and cultivating relationships using positive communication can provide motivation for members to work toward team success. A person's motivation is a combination of desire and energy directed at achieving a goal. Influencing someone's motivation means getting them to want to do what you know needs to be done. Team building can set the stage for a cohesive team that is motivated to work together to use the available resources to reach a particular goal.

You, the leader, must guide the group in deciding on the specific resources needed to reach certain goals. A decision needs to be made on where and when each resource will be needed, and who will be responsible for providing, acquiring, and scheduling each resource. As a leader, you may not always know what is needed; however, good leaders will make a deliberate effort to identify specific resources that are needed to reach the goals as they listen to group discussions.

Some key points motivating people and making correct allocations are:

- Know and respect people's education, skills, and abilities.

- Show people you have confidence in their abilities to do a job right.

- Give people a whole job – not a series of doled-out tasks.

- Give people ownership of jobs, tell them what needs to be done, let them decide how to do it, then back off.

- Give feedback on how they are doing (but do not look over their shoulders).

- Recognize people publicly for their achievements.

A good leader needs to be able to delegate effectively. You cannot do everything. The key to delegating successfully is giving people ownership of the work they are doing. Let your group know that you will be there for them through the good and the bad times.

Delegating Pointers:

- Delegating responsibilities is a critical part of being a good leader.

- Clarify and agree on the amount of control each person will have.

- The best way to lead people is to give them the ability to lead themselves.

- Create a work environment in which there is mutual support, mutual trust, and genuine lines of communication.

- Clarify what decisions individuals can make without reporting to the leader.

- Agree on the events that would constitute failure.

Leaders who decide to make decisions with the participation of the group members do so because they feel that this results in high quality decisions for which they are willing to be accountable. The effective leader and group will build specific procedures for evaluating their own effectiveness, and will be accountable for the functions and responsibilities they assume. Knowing they have had input on how the group will carry out tasks will also motivate members to go above and beyond assigned tasks to ensure the group achieves its goals. The leader will always have the ultimate accountability for the success or failure of the group in reaching the goals that have been set, but chances of success increase with the levels of motivation in the group.

Exercise

Think of past teams or groups you have been a part of. What motivated you to participate and complete the assigned task? List 5 things that motivated you and why you think they worked. Also put a check if you think they would work with others.

MOTIVATION TABLE

What motivated you?	Why did it motivate you?	Will it work with others?
1.		
2.		
3.		
4.		
5.		

Collaboration

People more readily accept new ideas and new methods of doing things when they are given the opportunity to participate in making the decisions that affect the group. One of the principle benefits to group members from having a leader who makes it possible for them to participate in group problem solving and decision-making is that this activity gives them the opportunity to satisfy their social and interactional needs, their needs for self-esteem and status in the organization, and even their needs for self-actualization and self-development. The leader also gains more insight into the needs of the group members. Individual members of an organization will be more identified with the goals of the group, and more concerned about its success if they participate in making decisions about those goals and how to reach them. An effective leader must be perceived as another group member so that group members will feel free to contribute to the group. All contributions should be evaluated on merit, not on prestige.

Allow your group to be part of the planning and problem solving process. This helps them to become owners of the process, and gives them a personal interest in seeing things succeed. When people pull together and collaborate to create solutions that work, everyone wins.

Some important things to remember:

- Recognize publicly for improved or outstanding performance.

- To the extent possible, give tangible rewards.

- Give new challenges and opportunities when they are ready to tackle them.

- Let people know when their performance is not up to par.

- Counsel when necessary on how they can improve their performance (offer tangible aids).

- Be clear about your expectations.

The Team

The team, which includes the leader, is the result of an effective leader building a team by using positive communication to motivate members to collaborate to achieve the goals of the group. It doesn't matter how many people are in the group; what matters is whether or not they feel needed and valued for their contributions. The expression, "You get more bees with honey than vinegar," can be applied to team building. When a leader gives the team the tools and support to be successful, the team will meet, and often times exceed the expectations of the leader. An effective leader is really a facilitator of the group. They keep the group on target to achieve the goals, without steamrolling over the other members. Team building by creating and cultivating relationships will do more to motivate and encourage collaboration in a group than simply telling people what to do. Although some people prefer to be told what to do, they will appreciate the group experience much more if they are given some control and ownership in the group. The best leaders know this leads to their own success.

Notes:

_____

_____

_____

_____

_____

_____

_____

_____

_____

_____

_____

_____

_____

_____

_____

_____

_____

_____

_____

_____

_____

_____

_____

_____

ABOUT THE AUTHOR

CAROL HEADY

Carol Heady is founder and president of Learning and Performance Solutions, a consulting practice specializing in professional skills training, management and leadership development programs, organizational development, and coaching. Carol's passion and niche is helping professional women, women business owners and entrepreneurs further develop their leadership and business management capabilities to accelerate personal growth and achieve greater business success. This is done through customized individual and group coaching programs, as well as public seminars and teleseminars. She brings 25 years business experience from a diverse background including: financial services, retail, and telecommunications.

Carol has an undergraduate degree in education and obtained her M.S. in Organizational Management and Human Resources from Manhattanville College. She is an Adjunct Professor at Manhattanville College where she teaches a graduate course on corporate training and development, and is a certified facilitator for three international training companies: Achieve Global, Omega Performance and Development Dimensions International. Carol is President of the Westchester/Mid-Hudson Chapter of American Society for Training and Development. She is a member of several professional associations including: International Coach Federation, Society of Human Resources Management, Toastmasters International, The Professional Woman Speakers Bureau, and the PWN International Advisory Board.

Contact:
Carol A. Heady, President
Learning and Performance Solutions
29 Ridge Road
Hopewell Junction, NY 12533
845-226-8047
www.learningandperformance.net
carol@learningandperformance.net

FIFTEEN

BEING A MORE SELF-AWARE LEADER

By Carol Heady

Becoming a more self-aware leader means understanding yourself from the inside out. I often refer to this critical dimension of successful leadership as your intra-personal compass. Where does self-awareness come from? In large part, it comes from your experiences, relationships, environment, belief system and values. This creates our view of life, or our "life's filters". In other words, it's 100% who you are, so the greater the understanding you have of yourself, the more successful you will be at understanding others, and influencing others effectively. Your intra-personal compass represents how you feel and think in situations, and helps you make effective decisions about yourself and others, particularly during challenging or difficult situations. In other words, this helps you stay in tune with your emotions, and how you tend to respond to specific situations and people.

Self-awareness can be defined as your ability to accurately assess your strengths and weaknesses, and helps you to have a deep understanding of your emotions in different situations. This includes recognizing your talents, what you may need to develop or compensate for, and how you may need to adapt to different situations and people. Identifying the gap becomes a starting point for change. The beauty of being a more self-aware leader is that it enables you to make positive changes towards personal growth and development, and in turn, will have a positive impact on others.

Developing your self-awareness requires a desire to understand your strengths and recognize how you react and feel in situations and interactions with others. With a heightened sense of self-awareness you begin understanding how your behaviors and how you communicate influences others. Utilizing your heightened sense of awareness enables you to make more thoughtful decisions and leverage your talents to experience greater opportunity for success. In addition, being a more self aware leaders also enables you to be more mindful of other's thoughts, ideas, and feelings and stretches you to detach from your "life's filters" (perceptions/feelings/bias') while listening to others so that you can remain objective and non-judgmental.

Understanding your limitations and where you may need to compensate or develop yourself is equally important to developing your self-awareness. Just as you will leverage your strengths, knowing how to compensate for your weakness is very empowering. This recognition alone will propel you to examine the strengths in others and begin maximizing their strengths to lead more effectively. Other times it will be in your best interest and the interest of others to develop a particular skill, change a behavior or attitude. For example, if you receive feedback that you do not demonstrate effective interpersonal communication skills or team building skills, obviously you would want to focus on developing these skills as opposed to relying on someone else to do this for you. On the other hand, if you find your analytical abilities specifically with numbers (ex. generating statistical reports, analyzing trends) is not a strength, and that talent exists in another person this is when compensating for your weakness may be a smart use of leveraging the other person's abilities. You may want to delegate that particular task.

Key Indicators

There are several key indicators that demonstrate being a more self-aware leader:

- **Self-alignment**: know who you are and what you believe in

- **Self-knowledge**: recognizes and openly acknowledges one's own leadership strengths and weaknesses

- **Self motivated**: takes action to leverage strengths and develop or compensate for weaknesses to achieve desired results

- Confidently **expresses** own **values**, beliefs and vision

- Recognition of one's **leadership style**, behavioral and communication preferences

- Recognizes that people have **different styles** and preferences and is willing to flex or adapt her style as required

- Appreciation for **diversity,** and the ideas, opinions, and beliefs of others

- Actively elicits **feedback** and is adaptable and open to new ideas

- Takes time to reflect on **self-knowledge** and elicited feedback to build on strengths and develop or compensate for weaknesses

- Never stops **learning** about self and others

Increasing Self-Awareness

Inquiry and reflection are two of the most effective techniques to develop and increase self-awareness. There are different "tools" designed to help people increase their self-awareness using inquiry and reflection. I will share a few with you; before I do I believe a critical first step to increasing self-awareness is willingness. A willingness to examine ourselves and the perception of others, to embrace and receive feedback, followed by leveraging that increased self awareness to make the desired changes. An increase in self-awareness is a beautiful thing, it allows you to discover what you want to continue doing, stop doing and start doing. This enables you to grow and change to experience greater success.

Here is one exercise (tool) that can help you examine your "life's filters". I call it **"Your Life's Influences"** using inquiry and reflection. This is designed to begin the process of examining where your beliefs, values, and perceptions come from. These are rooted in your most influential life experiences (family, education, religion, occupation, volunteerism, etc.). The circle in the center of the diagram represents "You". The surrounding circles represent the most influential life experiences that have shaped who you are. Take the time to reflect on who and/or what these experiences are and why they were so influential. As you think about these experiences begin to fill in the outer circles with names, places, etc., use a piece of paper to write down all the thoughts and feelings that come to you for each one. Once you have captured your thoughts and feelings ask yourself these questions:

- What insight have I gained about myself?

- How do these influences impact or affect my role as leader?

- Who would I be willing to share this with and why?

- When will I share it?

Exercise: Your Life's Influences

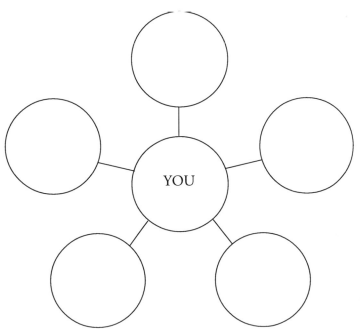

Another "tool" to increase self-awareness is an assessment instrument. Assessing your strengths and weaknesses is truly an empowering experience that will increase your self-awareness exponentially. There are two types of assessments. One is a self-assessment, and the other is what's called a multi-rater assessment, or **360 Degree Feedback**. A self-assessment tool is designed for you to assess yourself openly and honestly. A multi-rater assessment is designed for you to elicit feedback from others to evaluate your leadership competencies anonymously. With a multi-rater assessment, you are typically eliciting feedback from your peers, boss, and direct reports (clients or customers can also be included), and a certified professional with the chosen 360 Degree instrument administers the feedback and results. The greatest value with a multi-rater assessment is that you are getting the perception of those you interact and communicate with. Both are valuable tools to increase your self-awareness, and both require open, honest feedback. An important aspect of maximizing the value of multi-rater assessments is having the willingness and openness to receive the feedback and leveraging that information to maximize strengths, identify developmental opportunities, and make desired changes.

One typed of self-assessment tool is referred to as a **"SWOT" Analysis**. This can be a starting point to begin the self-assessment process. A "SWOT" assesses your **S**trengths, **W**eaknesses, **O**pportunities, and **T**hreats. This process helps you recognize and take advantage of your talents and abilities, and uncover opportunities to leverage those talents, as well as identifying your weaknesses and any threats that may exist that would catch you unaware. In other words, this will help you uncover potential challenges or obstacles to increasing your self-awareness. The beauty of this process is that it enables you to pre-empt obstacles and uncover "blind spots". To perform a mini Personal

"SWOT" assessment to enhance your self-awareness, write down answers to the questions below. It is important to be open and honest with yourself as you answer these questions.

Exercise: Personal SWOT Assessment
Strengths

What do you consider your leadership strengths?

How do you leverage those strengths?

What do others see as your strengths?

What technical knowledge/skills do you possess/leverage?

What functional expertise/experience do you possess/leverage?

Weaknesses

What skills, behaviors, or knowledge would you like to develop?

What would you like to stop doing?

What would you like to do better?

Opportunities (Positive external conditions/factors that you don't necessarily control, but you can leverage)

What opportunities do you have to elicit feedback on your leadership competencies?

What opportunities do you have to leverage other people's strengths?

What are the opportunities to create value for the ideas and opinions of others?

Threats (Negative external conditions/factors that you don't necessarily control, but you may be able to overcome)

What obstacles or challenges would you face to elicit feedback?

What might prevent you from leveraging other people's strengths?

What might prevent you from leveraging your leadership strengths?

Once you have answered the questions, spend some time reflecting on the answers and how you will take action on your new insights. Think about who you might want to share the insights with and what you want to begin focusing on. It is important to focus on one aspect of your "SWOT" assessment at a time. In the absence of a formally administered 360 degree instrument, you can elicit feedback on area's you would like to gain further insight using the "SWOT" questions, or other questions specific to what you would like further insight on. For example, you could ask people: What do you consider to be my leadership strengths? Another question might be: In my leadership role, what do you want me to do more of? And, what do you want me to stop doing? These are powerful, insightful questions. The other aspect of doing this type of exercise is that you are demonstrating that you value people's feedback. This requires courage and trust, and a certain amount of risk and vulnerability. The reward is gaining insight on what I call our "blind spots". If you are unaware of how your behaviors, perceptions, attitudes, leadership and communication styles affect how you influence others, then you don't know how to adapt or change what you do to be a more effective leader.

Another powerful "tool" to increase self-awareness that uses the technique of inquiry and reflection is professional development coaching. The essence of coaching is raising awareness and increasing responsibility for the desired outcome or change. The process of coaching is facilitating change with individuals who are open to learning, introspection, self-reflection, and receiving feedback. From this process, you can experience a deeper understanding of your personal bias' and perceptions, identify what particular habit or behavior you want or need to change, and build greater trust and belief in yourself and others, to name a few. Developing self-awareness through coaching is invaluable from two perspectives. First, is that you will increase your own self-awareness, and that will serve you well with the second perspective, which is that you will coach and help develop others more effectively.

In addition to willingness, there are two other critical aspects of developing your self-awareness. They are taking action and not operating in a vacuum. You can look at developing self-awareness as a process, and taking action becomes step two in the process. The willingness to gather feedback and be introspective and reflective is vital (Step 1), but is not as useful if you don't take action on what you learn. The real growth or deeper understanding comes from what you do with what you have learned (Step 2). Think about the last time you discovered something about yourself whether through self discovery or the result of feedback from others and how you felt during that "Ah, ha" moment. (This is very valuable). Then think about what you did with that discovery, how you changed a behavior, an attitude, a viewpoint or handled a situation differently as a result of acting on your increased awareness. (This is very powerful and sometimes life altering.) None of that happened in a vacuum. The undeniable value of deepening your own level of self-awareness leads to better self-management, and increased effectiveness in interacting and communicating with others— essentially your relationship with people.

Some Parting Thoughts

Your intra-personal compass is your guide to understanding yourself from the inside out. As you deepen your level of understanding from an internal perspective, it will help you make more informed decisions and choices. This is an ongoing process that requires intention and constant attention, and comes with huge rewards for you and those you lead. Some of those rewards include:

• Increased self confidence

• Empowers you to make better decisions for yourself and others

• Empowers you to make better choices for yourself

• Empowers you to make changes to be more effective personally and professionally

• Increased flexibility with different individuals' behavioral preferences and styles

• Greater adaptability in different situations

• Experience greater success at achieving desired outcomes

• Increased trust and confidence in relationships

• Enhances your ability to influence and inspire others

• The ability to leverage personal strengths, and the talents of others to achieve greater success

Whether you are in a leadership role or preparing for one, I hope what I have shared will serve you well both personally and professionally.

Resources

Books and Articles
The Platinum Rule, by Dr. Tony Alessandra

Emotional Intelligence and Job Function, by Dr. Travis Bradberry and Lac D. Su

Primal Leadership: realizing the power of emotional intelligence, by Daniel Goleman

In Search of the Perfect Leader, by Libby McCready, Certified Business Coach

Leadership Skills and Emotional Intelligence, by The Center for Creative Leadership

Increasing EQ Through Coaching, by D. Paul Warner, M.S.

Professional Development Programs
Women and Leadership: What's Your Strategy for Success?, by Carol Heady, M.S. and Rita Weiss

Assessment Tools
DISC ® Inscape Publishing

What's My Leadership Style © HRDQ Research and Development Team, Organization and Development Inc.

ABOUT THE AUTHOR

PAMELA THOMPSON

Ms. Thompson's nearly thirty years' experience in education spans teaching grades K through 12, guidance counseling and administration. She has instructed in literature, public speaking, writing, and drama. Her strengths are in research, development and presentation, and she has been recognized for her work in professional development and incentive programs. A self-taught artist, Ms. Thompson enjoys teaching other adults to draw as well as continuing to develop her own skills, recently winning a regional award for mixed media art.

Thompson is a new addition to the PWN family and is in the process of developing a seminar business geared to the boomer generation going through new transitions. In addition, she plans to offer her writing and artistic skills to other PWN members by editing, revising, ghost writing and illustrating their self-published books. Her long range plans include a conference retreat center available to PWN members, business clients and the local community.

Ms. Thompson brings experience, knowledge and entertaining wit to her presentations, accessing the mind-body-spirit connection while managing to stay grounded and practical in her approach.

Contact:
Pamela Thompson
25 Indian Hill Drive
Crittenden, KY 41030
thompson.pam@insightbb.com
www.protrain.net

SIXTEEN

SETTING BOUNDARIES, NOT LIMITS

By Pamela Thompson

As an artist I find nothing more exciting (and intimidating) than facing a blank canvas. With the first brave strokes, however, fear subsides and joy ensues. I particularly enjoy mixed media art. For me that canvas has no limits, but it does have boundaries. Outside the dimensions of the canvas is chaos. If you don't believe me just look at the floor of my studio!

Living quite near the Bluegrass Region of Kentucky, I often admire the grand race horses secure behind miles of pristine white fences. Some may think it cruel to pen up any animal, but these horses run and roam over vast acres protected from traffic and predators, inoculated against diseases, and housed against the elements. (They even have swimming pools!) Clearly boundaries and limits don't mean the same thing.

In your personal and professional life I am certain that you want to soar, limitless, but to do so you need boundaries to prevent chaos or disaster from intruding. It is easy to allow other people or situations to invade our space and postpone or prevent us from achieving our goals. Only **you** can determine who or what, and when, you will allow access to your precious space and time. Let's first consider your personal life.

Exercise #1A

Personal Access: Using the following terms, place them in the appropriate column based upon **your current behavior with** *spouse, children, pets, parents, in-laws, friends (specific), hobbies, health, finances, chores, leisure activities, phone calls, travel, TV, etc.* Be as specific as you like.

EASY ACCESS	LIMITED ACCESS

As you review your completed lists, analyze what you see. Are you giving easy access to people (neighbors) or situations (TV) that are not of primary importance to you or your goals? Are you limiting people (spouse) or situations (hobbies) when they are of real value to you? Is it time to shift some boundaries?

Exercise #2A

Professional Access: Let's try the same exercise with your professional life and your **current behavior with**: *boss, staff (specific), phone calls, travel, paper work, meetings, appointments, interruptions, lunch, etc.* If you work from home, you may have others such as children or personal phone calls which invade your boundaries.

EASY ACCESS	LIMITED ACCESS

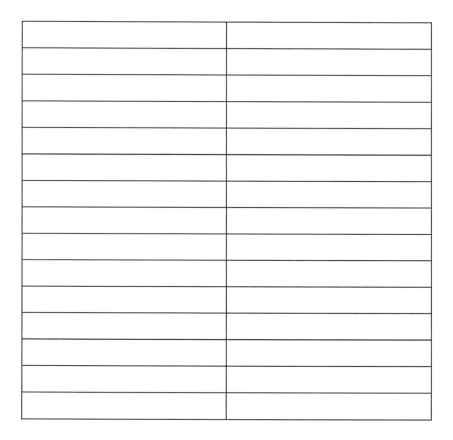

Once again, analyze your results. If you have several under EASY ACCESS and you are feeling stressed or unable to accomplish your goals, you definitely need to set some new boundaries at work. On the job, especially, you need to be in control of your day as much as is humanly possible.

With these ideas in mind, redo the above exercises in the spaces below based on **who and what you WANT** to give access to your time and space, in light of what you have learned. You may want to break them down even further into more specific detail.

For example, there are times when your children should have easy access to you, and times when they shouldn't. Some interruptions at work can be ignored. Some require immediate attention. Use your wise discretion.

Exercise #1B
Personal Access for the Future: New Boundaries and Limits In Your Personal Life

EASY ACCESS	LIMITED ACCESS

Exercise #2B

Professional Access for the Future: New Boundaries and Limits in Your Professional Life

EASY ACCESS	LIMITED ACCESS

Now that you have rethought your personal and professional boundaries, another important consideration is the <u>overlapping</u> of these two areas. It is wise to create a clear distinction between personal and professional areas, even if only in your mind, in order to avoid extreme stress and the deterioration of personal and work relationships.

As a high school English teacher, I brought home lesson plans and papers to grade, and I made parent phone calls in the evening. Though the general public expects this, it is not conducive to a healthy home life. Important relationships and responsibilities were being ignored. Problems developed. Later, when my husband and I taught in the same school, the problems worsened. Our personal lives went to school. Our professional lives came home. Only a good dose of counseling helped us both set boundaries. Eventually, all papers were graded at school, even if it meant staying late, or telling students the test would not be returned as promptly as they wanted. When the school day ended, my husband and I discussed school issues on the ride home. Once inside, school was not a topic. Our relationship and our mental health improved immediately, as did our attitudes about our jobs.

Below are two checklists. The first is for **issues at home that you bring to work.** (By mentally focusing on and being distracted, by discussing unprofessionally, etc.) The second is for issues **at work that you bring home.** (By constantly stressing over or discussing, etc.) Place a checkmark by all that apply. Add others to the lists that come to mind.

PERSONAL ISSUES I TAKE TO WORK	
	Money worries
	Health concerns
	Marriage/Relationship problems
	Parenting issues
	Addictions
	Family problems
	Other:

PROFESSIONAL ISSUES I BRING HOME	
	Office gossip
	Judgment toward others
	Perceived mistreatment
	Criticism of boss, coworkers, etc.
	Pay issues
	Unfair practices, demands
	Harassment
	Coworkers' personal/professional problems
	Other:

Let's be honest. We all discuss our home life over lunch and our work life over dinner. That is to be expected. However, your personal money worries, for instance, are better discussed at home, while your request for a raise to help in that regard should be dealt with at work.

When you find this "overlapping" becoming the norm, when it begins to adversely affect home and work relationships, it is time to look closely again at boundaries. It may be time to see a debt consolidation counselor to help relieve money worries. It may be time to ask for that raise or update that job resume. There are always better choices than to suffer in silence, or verbally annoy family and co-workers into stressful responses!

OK, Now What?

Well, you have now determined that you need to reestablish (or ESTABLISH) new boundaries. You know the who, the what, the when...but HOW? Yes, the next task is to communicate these boundaries and stay strong and focused. Usually it is the result of the awareness of the need to set boundaries that first makes us face *our lack of assertiveness*.

If you feel that others take advantage of you, don't listen to you, or don't allow you time for yourself, then you are admitting that your boundaries are under siege. If standing up for yourself is a new practice and those around you are accustomed to having their way, you may find it helpful to seek a counselor, a minister, or a life coach to assist and encourage you. However, I have been particularly aided by some excellent books on assertiveness, the classic being *The Assertive Woman* by Stanlee Phelps and Nancy Austin, recently revised and updated for the 21st century. Like the PWN series of books, it is hands-on and interactive, asking the hard questions and moving the reader to leave her comfort zone (which is actually quite uncomfortable), and to communicate effectively. The following list of suggestions will hopefully be helpful, as well:

Suggestions For Communicating Boundaries

1. **Don't try to tackle all of your boundaries at once.** Start with one or two at home and at work. Pick ones with which you can feel some immediate success. This will increase your confidence and set the groundwork for other changes, in your mind and the minds of others.

2. **Find an appropriate time and place for discussion with those concerned.** Don't try this as the kids dash out the door to school or hubby is watching football.

3. **Gently and firmly remind those involved the first few times— and follow through.** "Sorry, Mom, but I can't talk now. Remember, this is dinnertime. I'd love to chat, though. I'll call you tomorrow. When would be a good time?" This example also honors her time and space.

4. **Be polite and professional as you announce new policies, honoring everyone involved.** "From now on, my secretary will make all of my appointments to avoid conflicts and respect your valuable time."

5. **Take care of yourself FIRST.** This is tough for women. Some even feel it selfish or wrong. But, if you do not have the emotional, mental, physical or spiritual stamina you need first, how can you possibly help others? When a spouse feels threatened, a child feels ignored, a coworker thinks you have an "attitude", you can reassure them and kindly explain how this will actually give them MORE special time with you in the long run.

6. **Realize that some people may never accept the changes and that letting go may be in your future.** That's why we don't always start with the "biggies" unless your health, safety or sanity is at risk. It's important to remember that you can't be a Superwoman, nor should you be. You overextend yourself, and you cripple those dependent on you. Your life is your life, not your husband's, your mother's , your child's or your church's. Ultimately, a choice may have to be made, but you do NOT have to make any choice before you are ready.

7. **You are already good enough, and you already have all that you need inside you.** How I used to cringe every time I heard this. "I am not and I do not!!" I argued most vehemently. Turns out, it's true. It may take some time to scrape through the gunk, but the nugget is there. You betcha!

I once knew a professional woman who set absolutely NO boundaries in her business life. Home was virtually ignored, her office was pandemonium, and nothing of value was ever accomplished. What could have been an impressive career ended prematurely as, in her effort to please everyone, she "helped" an employee by compromising the company's ethics. She had grand goals and noble causes on her side, and the personality to succeed admirably; yet, her inability to assertively establish herself as the leader by setting boundaries, limited and, finally, squelched her wonderful vision.

SO...

Whether you are starting out in your career or making a transition, take a serious look at boundaries. When they are secure, your potential is limitless. Run wild and free behind the pristine white fences you have set to keep yourself securely focused on your goals; and fill the canvas of life with creative variety, making your life the work of art it was truly meant to be.

Suggested Reading

Overcoming the Superwoman Syndrome by Linda Ellis Eastman, ed. Prospect, KY: Professional Woman Publishing. 2007

The Assertive Woman by Stanlee Phelps and Nancy Austin, San Luis Obispo, CA: Impact Publishers. 1997

The Princessa: Machiavelli For Women by Harriet Rubin, Dell Publishing: New York, NY 1997

Notes:

_____

_____

_____

_____

_____

_____

_____

_____

_____

_____

_____

_____

_____

_____

_____

_____

_____

_____

_____

_____

ABOUT THE AUTHOR

KARYN E. TAYLOR

Karyn E. Taylor is President and founder of The Whole Self Design Consulting Group, which is dedicated to inspiring and motivating growth in individuals and organizations through seminars, training, workshops, consulting, and coaching.

Karyn is a member of the Professional Woman Network (PWN) and is a certified trainer in Diversity and Women's Issues, Professional Presentation Skills, and Career Coaching through the PWN.

Karyn's expertise in the areas of Diversity, Leadership, and Career and Success Coaching has given her the opportunity to empower and enrich the lives of others at work, at church and in her community. Ms. Taylor is the Volunteer Coordinator for the Pittsburgh Child Guidance Foundation. She is a member of Toastmasters International, and a volunteer Victim/Offender Mediator with the Pittsburgh Mediation Center.

Ms. Taylor completed her Bachelors of Arts Degree in Legal Studies at the University of Pittsburgh and her Master of Arts Degree in Industrial and Labor Relations at Indiana University of Pennsylvania. She has an extensive background in Human Services and Human Resources.

Karyn would like to thank her mother and mentor Dr. Elayne Arrington, for all of her support, guidance and inspiration. Linda Ellis Eastman, President of PWN, and Nyda Bittmann-Neville, President of TNB Consulting are Karyn's mentors as well. Karyn also acknowledges the contributions of Aldine Coleman, and Erica Elayne Taylor-Jones to this project.

Contact
Karyn E. Taylor
The Nuin Center
5655 Bryant Street
Pittsburgh, PA 15206
(412) 235-1739

SEVENTEEN

HOW TO BUILD A WINNING TEAM!

By Karyn Elayne Taylor

"Teamwork is the ability to work together toward a common vision, the ability to direct individual accomplishments towards organizational objectives. It is the fuel that allows common people to attain uncommon results." —Andrew Carnegie

Modern culture continues to become more fluid and dynamic. Factors contributing to this include the communications revolution, the global market, and the ever-increasing specialization and division of labor. The effect is that individuals are now required to work with many different groups of people in their professional and personal lives.

Teams of one type or another dominate today's work place. To move ahead or to hold on to our jobs, or even to start our own businesses, most of us are compelled to spend at least part of our time in collaborative effort. Consider the following teams:

Professional	Personal
Management Teams	Personal Support Networks
Task Forces or Committees	Professional Organizations
Project Teams	Church Group Teams
Quality Work Teams	Athletic Teams
Virtual Teams	Business Growth Networks

For the next few minutes, we will discuss teams and building teams. My hope is that, as you answer the questions presented, more questions will emerge. In the questioning and answering, I believe that you will identify strategies to assist you in being a winning team player and a winning team builder.

So far, I have used the word "team" or a form of it ten times. How would you define "team"?

_____

_____

_____

What do you think of when you hear the word "team"?

_____

_____

_____

Does the word lead you to remember positive experiences?

_____

_____

_____

I imagine that as adults we have each experienced teams and teamwork at our best and our worst. Please document your experiences in the space provided. Indicate your feelings, whether or not you felt supported, and if there was a team member who could have assisted in turning each of these experiences around.

Worst Case	
In-Between Case	
Best Case	

I appreciate all of your hard work thus far. I know that these answers may be difficult to express, but your answers provide the foundation for determining:

- What you need from your participation in teams.

- What your teammates might need from you.

- Ways in which you need to experience and provide support.

What do you see as benefits of participating on a team?

Examples:

- Teamwork improves the working environment.

- Teamwork relieves stress.

- Teamwork keeps the lines of communication open.

- Teamwork reduces errors.

- Teamwork allows for shared responsibility.

_____

_____

_____

I know that we are devoting our time to the positive side of teams; however, we know from dreadful interactions that teams can actually be dysfunctional. They can produce bad decisions, they can be disruptive, and they can actually be wasteful of people's time and energy. For two absolutely wonderful discussions on how to deal with the dysfunctional aspects of teams, see Lencioni (Pg.187-220) and Butterfield (Pg. 18-50) listed in the resources section.

How do we know that the team is operating effectively or winning? I propose that we use, at the very least, four criteria to determine if the team experience is a winning one.

Was the team output judged to meet or exceed the expectations of the people who received the output? Were the customers' needs met?

Is the team able to function within the organization or framework effectively after they have completed their task? After the team has separated, do the team members have an enhanced working relationship that benefits the group or organization?

Does the team feel satisfied with their efforts? If the team members themselves are pleased with their results, if the experience has been a good experience, if the time spent away from their usual work has been worth the effort, the team has likely to probably been effective.

Did the team meet its overall goals and the individual needs of each teammate? Teams must respond to the needs of the organization and the needs of the members.

Perhaps you can add a few criteria of your own

_____

_____

_____

_____

_____

_____

Characteristics of a Winning Team

- Everyone is supportive of the project and of others.

- Everyone participates actively and positively.

- Everyone takes responsibility for getting things done.

- Everyone takes initiative to get things done.

- Team goals are understood by everyone.

- Team goals are given realistic time frames.

- Team members are willing to take risks.

- Team members communicate with each other.

- Team members trust the judgments of the others.

- Team decisions are made using organized logical methods.

"There is no "I" in 'Team'." —Unknown

I heard the expression, "There is no "I" in 'team'." about six years ago. As I recall, the circumstance was after an incredibly horrible staff meeting in which we, of course, started 20-30 minutes late. We did not follow the agenda, and there was seemingly no clear reason for why we met at all, except that Thursday afternoon at 3:00 pm was our scheduled staff meeting time. We did not get released from the meeting until 5:00 pm, and I knew that I was going to (really, this time) begin the process of looking for another place of employment. One of my co-workers and I would often take walks after the staff meeting. This Thursday we walked and talked for a very long time, way past 6:00 pm. I don't remember being in a bad mood, but I imagine I must have been angry, frustrated, and overwhelmed as I often was after staff meetings. What I do remember is that as we parted company, he was half way across the parking garage when I heard him call my name in a very concerned voice. As I turned toward him, I heard him say, "Karyn, remember there is no 'I' in 'team'."

What does that mean? All right, two points for him, and an additional point to ponder. Everyone knows and can see that there is no "I" in "team"; At the time, I really took this to mean that I was expecting and giving too much of myself; I wanted to take on everything; that I truly believed I could handle it all its been said "If you want it done right, you have to do it yourself." I took this to mean that I could and should expect more from my coworkers. These six words caused me to evaluate my work and working environment. The words caused me to think, feel, and then define team. For me, **a team is a small number of people with complementary skills who are committed to a common purpose, common performance goals, and a common approach for which they hold themselves mutually accountable.**

Today, as I read the words "there is no 'I' in 'team'", I understand the expression in a different way. The word "team" does not contain the letter i, but the essential element of a team is an **individual**. I see this as what I bring to the team – those elements that make me unique – how I think, my attitude, my energy, and also what I do. As a team member, I have to focus (and stay focused) on how

- **I** believe in our team purpose.

- **I** contribute to the performance goals.

- **I** approach my work and my teammates.

- **I** hold myself accountable for how I respond and contribute to the group process.

My new approach is to recognize that as team members we each have needs. We each have the need to belong, the need to feel worthy, and the need to feel competent. This fundamental shift has caused me to look at each of my coworkers and other team members in a new light. I respect them for who they are and how they act. I recognize that we got to the same place for different reasons and in different ways, but I believe that each one of us wants the very best for each of the "customers" we serve.

The staff meetings often start late. The agenda is often not followed. We almost never get out of the meetings on time, and **I** now know that **I** work with a good group of committed, supportive people, and I am proud to be a part of our team. Thank you, Hassan for helping release my resentments by recognizing the need to turn them into respect.

"Individual commitment to a group effort…that is what makes a team work, a company work, a society work, a civilization work."
—Vince Lombardi

When we are asked to participate on a team, to assist in accomplishing some task, immediately our decision making process begins. We have to decide what kind of commitment we are willing to make. Use the following questions to guide you through your assessment. These questions should relate to both your professional and personal experiences.

What is the purpose of the team or task?

Who will be on the team with me?

Is it important to management?

Will I have any authority?

Does this fit with my individual purpose?

What is the risk for not participating?

Is this a topic that interests me?

What is the reward for participating?

How much time will I have to commit?

Will I be better off as a result of my participation?

Characteristics of a Winning Team Member

- Understands and is committed to team objectives.

- Does not engage in win/ lose activities with other team members.

- Has an understanding of what is going on within the group.

- Encourages feedback on her or his own behavior.

- Respects and is tolerant of individual differences.

- Encourages the development of other team members.

- Acknowledges and works through conflict openly.

- Involves others in the decision making process.

- Influences others by involving them in the issue(s).

- Appreciates and uses new ideas from others.

The Six A's of Building a Winning Team

1. Accomplish

In building the winning team, we need to be clear about what we want to accomplish. This is the key to success. The team needs a team generated, simply stated objective that each member understands and can see as achievable.

The plan to improve the quality or effectiveness of the team must contain:

- **The objective** – This objective must be aligned with the purpose, mission, vision and values of the organization, and provide a clear sense of direction.

- **The method** – A plan of action can be developed once the approach to the task is agreed upon. The team can develop goals and focus on the desired outcome!

- **The design for monitoring the outcome** – A way to measure the team progress is also necessary. This way the team can celebrate success at important milestones.

- **The criteria for completion** – Agreed upon criteria for project completion or curtailment must be established. The time spent getting all of the members on the same page will reduce the number of derailments or rerouting along the way.

2. Assign

Another critical issue is that of assigning members to the team. Before members are assigned, it is important to examine what each member brings to the task. For assignments to work best, we want to keep in mind the following three areas:

- **Selecting participants** – As the team leader, it is important to have team members that are able to build trust among the other participants. Sometimes it may be helpful to have participants complete an assessment at the beginning of the project and after the project completion.

- **Balancing skill sets** – When creating winning teams, it is important to have balanced skill sets. One way to achieve this is to have members with different areas of expertise come together. Individuals with people skills will work with people who have technical skills. By combining as many different skills as possible, the team will function at a level that benefits everyone. This seems very challenging to achieve, but important for ensuring the success of one's team.

- **Allocating roles within the team** – It is important to assign roles to team members so that each knows his or place on the team. Each role should relate to the team member's personality, and the role should be clearly defined. We must make sure people are assigned according to their talents, and avoid the temptation to assign people to a team for political or personal reasons.

3. Atmosphere

In order to engage the enthusiasm of the entire team, we must create the right atmosphere. The goal is to have an atmosphere that lends itself for participants to:

- **Communicate** – We must create an environment in which each member feels totally free to express an idea. In order to have effective communication within our team, it is crucial that an environment is maintained in which people feel free to talk about what concerns them. This can be done only if it is ok to be wrong. There must be no stigma attached to being incorrect. An idea is not wrong, simply not optimal. In each suggestion there may be a seed for future growth. Someone should point this out, and where possible, build upon it.

- **Team oriented language** – Another method that I like and that seems to work well is to constantly talk about Our Team in the plural pronoun: "We decided," "We can do this," "We will get back to you." This method builds camaraderie, and team members seem at ease, as they are able to present a unified front of mutual support.

- **Code of conduct** – A code of conduct must be agreed upon at the beginning of the project. The most critical rules pertain to attendance, approaches to problems, planning the work, and sharing the assignments. This will make sure that the work is done on time, and done well.

4. Approach

An important aspect of team interaction is the idea of mutual support. If we can instill the idea that all problems are owned by the entire team, then each member will be able to seek advice or support when needed from every other team member.

- **Mutual coaching** – As teams are built, we must look at all the relational aspects of being a participant. We have to recognize the

Up, Down, and Across of the entire experience. If one team member knows information that is useful to the rest of the team, then he or she should be encouraged to share the information. Likewise, all members should feel encouraged to ask questions and give information.

- **Experiencing coachable moments** – Team-builders recognize the opportunity for coaching, even in moments of what look like personal crisis. Athletic coaches make great use of the video replays of team performances, both good and bad, to assist the athletes in modifying, improving, or repeating their behaviors. These "stop and pause" portions of the training are "coachable" moments. "Sometimes, the biggest window for changing someone's self-concept opens when he or she fails." (In *Fast Company* Magazine, July 2001.)

Coachable moments come only at points of vulnerability, humility, hunger, fear, and need. Can you identify some coachable moments in your life when you were able to learn? Can you think of a recent coachable moment you experienced with a member of your team? What were the circumstances?

- **Instilling team spirit** – If we can participate in mutual coaching and allow ourselves at times to experience "coachable moments", some level of vulnerability on the way to achieving our team goals, then we have gone a very long way in instilling team spirit.

5. Action

How will the team accomplish its goals? The winning team must focus on results. As the team begins, they must set up guidelines and procedures for how they will get to the end result. Team builders can emphasize the impact of individual members on team productivity.

Also, they can clarify valued team member behaviors. Here, we want to look at three ideas: Follow through, Creativity and Spirit.

- **Follow-through** – On a winning team, members trust that when a colleague agrees to return a call, read a report, talk to a customer, or change a behavior, the job will be done. Team members are aware that everything they do, or don't do, impacts the team.

- **Creativity** – Originality flourishes on teams when individuals feel supported by their colleagues. Taking the lead in a new order of things is risky business; the risk is greatly reduced in a cooperative environment where members forgive mistakes, respect individual differences, and shift their thinking from a point of view to a viewing point.

- **Spirit** – Being on a team is very much like being part of a family. We do not get our way all of the time. We learn to forgive and accept forgiveness. So, in the spirit of teams, all of our actions need to value each individual, develop team trust, communicate openly, manage differences, share successes, and welcome new members.

6. Acknowledge

Rewards and recognition are important, and perhaps even mandatory. The team must recognize their value; and team leaders and management must also recognize the team's accomplishments.

- **Teamwork culture** – As leaders, we want to always promote the team's key strengths. We want to keep the team members aware of the ways in which they excel, or are above average. We want to use phrases that support teamwork. Where or when possible (during work time), we want to encourage team members to spend time together outside of the team working environment. Perhaps breakfast or lunch will do. Special cards or emails to thank each participant may be sent.

- **Emphasize group recognition** – We must find ways to increase pride in the group by broadcasting their successes through postings on company bulletin boards, or company newsletters.

- **Public** – There is a need to have celebrations/recognitions to mark the team's milestones. Give certificates and awards for the work that has been completed and is well done.

- **Private** – As team builders, we must help each team member appreciate the balance between being a good team player and finding room for individual recognition. We need to encourage and invite team members to be aware of how the team's accomplishments fit with their individual goals, and how they have benefited from the group process.

Team Creed

We will treat each member with respect.
We agree that every job is important.
We are diverse.
We will accept the challenge of unexpected opportunities.
We will look for ways to inspire and motivate each other.
We will look for ways to be more creative, rather than predictable.
We will let go of ideas that are not working.
We are one in our performance.

Summary

A key organizational, and perhaps personal, reality is that, to be successful, we have to be good team players. We have to build winning teams, as well. We must be clear about what we want to accomplish. We need to recruit the right people for the right position, at the right time, and for the right reason. We need to create an environment that allows positive interactions among the team members, and allows individual growth and development to occur. Surely, as team members and team builders, we each need to be accountable for helping each other reach our goals. We need to lead the cheering for each other. We need to expect the best in ourselves and others. As we build winning individuals, we are building winning teams. We must realize that teamwork can best be described in five simple yet powerful words – **We Believe in Each Other.**

Reading Resources

The Five Dysfunctions of a Team: A Leadership Fable by Patrick Lencioni

Tip for Teams: A Ready Reference for Solving Common Team Problems – Packed with 100's of Solutions! by Kimberly Fisher, Steven Rayner, and William Belgard

Teach Your Team to Fish Using Ancient Wisdom by Laurie Beth Jones

Building Successful Teams by Bill Butterworth

Unstuck: A Tool for Yourself, Your Team, and Your World by Yameshita Keith

Notes:

ABOUT THE AUTHOR

PAMELA COWAN

Pamela Cowan is the owner of a financial planning practice, Cowan Financial, LLC. Her key focus when working with clients is to educate and assist them in making better decisions in their lives especially as it relates to their finances.

Ms. Cowan is a graduate of the University of Toronto with a Bachelor of Commerce degree in Finance and Economics and a minor in Political Science. She has many years of experience as an accountant and later as a consultant in the computer software field which included international travel. In addition, she has conducted training for adults in accounting and computer applications. Her passion for teaching, led her to a career as a planner to be better able to assist and teach people on a more personal level.

Contact
Cowan Financial, LLC
2041 Stockmeyer Blvd.
Westland, MI 48186
(734) 722-5227
Pamela.A.Cowan@gmail.com

EIGHTEEN

PERSONAL STEPS TO FINANCIAL EMPOWERMENT

By Pamela Cowan

Em·pow·er: 1 : to give official authority or legal power to, 2 : enable, 3 : to promote the self-actualization or influence of (Merriam-Webster Dictionary) **Empowerment** refers to increasing the spiritual, political, social or economic strength of individuals and communities. It often involves the empowered developing confidence in *their own* (my emphasis) capacities. (Wikipedia, the free encyclopedia)

I absolutely love this definition of empowerment. It summarizes the topic, but also begs the question, "**Who** grants the empowerment?" The answer is that we grant it to ourselves. If that is true, then how do you know when you have achieved financial empowerment, and if you haven't, what is the strategy for obtaining it?

So, what does it feel like to be financially empowered? My unofficial definition would include more than simply making a great deal of money. The amount of money is completely subjective. What may constitute a good living for one may be inadequate for another. Many people who earn a good living don't necessarily feel empowered or satisfied with what they are doing, or may be missing a sense of fulfillment. Being empowered encompasses not only that you are living at a comfortable economic level, but that you also have acceptance of who you are, feel that you are doing or performing meaningful work, or are involved in activities that intrinsically feel successful to you. Some wish to be charitable, or to help their families, others feel comfort in the knowledge that they have adequate earnings to fund their futures.

I have chosen to explore this topic, merely scratching the surface, and my purpose is two-fold. First, I feel that many women are guilty of self-sabotage, consciously and sub-consciously, when it comes to advancement and being comfortable with making money. Second, I feel that fixing or adjusting your attitude involves more than using positive thoughts, affirmations and visualization. I concur with several authors and have found that the greatest change and release from past attitudes and history can best be achieved by recognizing where these beliefs have come from and addressing your past. Positive thinking that focuses on the future without addressing the past can only be compared to a 'seminar high'; we feel great after spending a day in a seminar, but it has no lasting effects.

I've included a quiz from Barbara Stanny's book, *Secrets of Six-Figure Women,* to help see if you are what she terms a chronic "Under-earner". Stanny's book focuses on identifying long- held beliefs and attitudes concerning money that we learned from family values and attitudes growing up. These attitudes often hold us back from earning what we are truly worth, and working in fields that actually interest us. Many of these beliefs are reinforced through our own experiences. Many of the women she interviewed were not aware that their long held beliefs and attitudes were costing them not only in direct earning power, but in peace of mind. Stanny is not the first author to proclaim this. Similar themes are included by authors in both the self-help and development realm from Stephen Covey to other financial writers, such as Suze Orman.

Women who have not addressed their money issues from their childhood are often, as Barbara Stanny labels it, chronic under-earners. They work for less money than they should and subconsciously sabotage their efforts to get ahead. Their excuses are endless and range from an expectation that they will be rescued, the "Prince Charming" syndrome, to a feigned dislike or belief that making money will somehow taint them or make them less noble in their chosen profession. In truth, making a decent living gives you more choices, peace of mind, and more opportunities to live a full life and to engage in philanthropic activities. Do you think Oprah Winfrey, now the most affluent woman in the United States, is tired of giving away money and helping others? Think again.

I am sure you are aware of an occasion where you have held yourself back from applying for a promotion, or making a change in your life that would have advanced your career, and ultimately your earning potential. Your reasons at the time may have been from a fear that more hours would have been involved or more responsibility. Perhaps it was even a sense that you didn't belong in the management level, which makes the conscious or subconscious decision even more insidious. The first step in this process, like any 12 step process, is to recognize that you have a problem. Only then can you begin to address and move on from these financially debilitating habits.

Quiz: Am I an Under-Earner?

Check the statements that apply to you. Do this quickly, without thinking too much about your response. Check the ones that might apply, even if you're not quite sure.	
	1. I often give away my services (volunteering, working more hours than actually paid).
	2. It's so hard to ask for a raise (or raise fees) that I just don't do it.
	3. I have negative feelings about money and/or wealthy people.
	4. I am proud of my ability to make do with little.
	5. Someone or something else (IRS, ex-husband) is responsible for my financial situation.
	6. I find ways to avoid dealing with money (bartering).
	7. I tend to sabotage myself at work (apply for jobs not qualified for or low-paying, stop short of reaching goals, change jobs a lot).
	8. I work very, very hard (long hours, several jobs). Or I go into excess and then collapse.
	9. I fill my free time with endless chores and tasks.
	10. I am in debt, with little savings, and no idea where my money is going.
	11. I have a family history of debt and/or under-earning.
	12. I am vague about my earnings (I overestimate or underestimate income; I see gross, not net).

	13. I continually put others' needs before my own.
	14. I am frequently in financial pain or stress.
	15. Recognition and praise are more important to me than money.
	16. I am confident in my ability to make money.
	17. I always live below my means.
	18. I love money and appreciate what it does for me.
	19. I am very optimistic about my financial future.
	20. I experience very little fear or insecurity around money.
	21. I am determined to get paid what I am worth.
	22. I am passionate about my work.
	23. I have very supportive, nurturing relationships (including spouse).
	24. I admire wealthy people.
	25. I have little or no credit card debt.
	26. I get myself in situations beyond my ability and then rise to them.
	27. I am resilient and able to bounce back when I fail.
	28. I am filled with gratitude for the success I've achieved.
	29. I work very hard, but I know I don't have to do everything myself. I know how to delegate and set limits.
	30. I am tenacious in achieving my goals.

Scoring: If you checked two or more of statements 1-15, you're probably earning less than your potential, despite your efforts and/ or desire to make more. If you checked two or more statements 16-30, you're likely in the upper-income brackets of your profession or industry.

Recognizing that you have some negative thoughts and feelings about money or about wealthy people may have been the easy part. For some, the recognition and realization will be enough to spur some inward healing, and start the process of moving on in your life. For others, more in depth work may be required.

Your personal financial empowerment has to come from more than just being able to do or afford something. Your internal satisfaction or power will come when you are doing something that you not only love, but that agrees with or is in line with your core values.

We often grow up and work at becoming what other people had planned for us. It's no wonder we achieve little satisfaction after years of schooling to get that 'dream' job. Whose dream? And we all do it. We are guilty of it with our own children as we try to direct them or their interests into fields where we think they will make a decent living and become a 'normal and productive' member of society; and we do this with the greatest sincerity.

First, I believe that you have been so conditioned that in some cases you no longer are aware of what you value as a person. Imagine working for years as a nurse if helping others or a caring attitude were not part of your internal make-up. It would be drudgery looking after sick people and performing day-to-day tasks for them that they are unable to do themselves. Would you want to be tended to by someone not of this mindset? Of course not, and people don't want to deal with you either when you are forcing yourself to act interested in a job that doesn't interest you. If you don't ever do the things that matter to you deeply, you will feel stressed. Therefore, it is important to explore inward to find out what really matters to you most. Take the Values exercise below. It may surprise you, and reignite some passions that you thought you had long buried.

Values Exercise
Begin this exercise by placing checkmarks next to all values that are important to you. If you notice some of your values are missing, add them in the blank spaces provided.

Core Values Identification List

❑ Achievement	❑ Fairness	❑ Order
❑ Advancement	❑ Fame	❑ Personal Development
❑ Adventure	❑ Family Happiness	❑ Personal Expression
❑ Affection	❑ Fast Living	❑ Playfulness
❑ Arts	❑ Fast-Paced Work	❑ Pleasure
❑ Autonomy	❑ Financial Gain	❑ Power
❑ Challenging Problems	❑ Freedom	❑ Privacy
❑ Change & Variety	❑ Friendship	❑ Purity
❑ Close Relationships	❑ Growth	❑ Quality
❑ Community	❑ Health	❑ Recognition
❑ Competence	❑ Helping Others	❑ Relationships
❑ Competition	❑ Helping Society	❑ Religion
❑ Completion	❑ Honesty	❑ Reputation
❑ Cooperation	❑ Independence	❑ Responsibility
❑ Collaboration	❑ Influencing Others	❑ Safety & Security
❑ Country	❑ Inner Harmony	❑ Self-Respect
❑ Creative Expression	❑ Integrity	❑ Serenity
❑ Decisiveness	❑ Intellectual Status	❑ Service
❑ Democracy	❑ Involvement	❑ Sophistication

❑ Diversity	❑ Job Tranquility	❑ Spirituality
❑ Ecological Awareness	❑ Knowledge	❑ Stability
❑ Economic Security	❑ Leadership	❑ Status
❑ Efficiency	❑ Loyalty	❑ Truth
❑ Equality	❑ Meaningful Work	❑ Wealth
❑ Ethical Practice	❑ Merit	❑ Wisdom
❑ Excellence	❑ Money	❑ Work Alone
❑ Excitement	❑ Nature	❑ Work on Frontiers
❑ Expertise	❑ Openness	❑ Work with Others
❑ _____	❑ _____	❑ _____
❑ _____	❑ _____	❑ _____

Look carefully at the items you have checked and then pick the top 10. From that list, pick the top 3. These are your core values.

Many think that sound finances and a good job lead to good health and well-being. Actually, it is the opposite. Most health professionals will tell you that the leading change in a person's health and well-being comes from a change in their attitude and outlook on life. It is the same with their finances. Numerous self-help books are dedicated to helping you think positive thoughts and to develop a healthy belief in yourself and your skills. But you need more than positive thoughts. You need to act. Setting goals, personally, professionally, and in line with your values, will be key. I would encourage you to keep reading as many of the self-help, feel good books as you can possibly devour. They all have marvelous insights, and like any topic which needs to be studied, finally one of them will say something in such a way that your 'aha' moment will arrive.

In addition to developing a healthy belief in yourself and a positive outlook, make peace with your past. In order to make use of the positive 'go forward' advice, we need to have a firm grasp to deal with why we feel we may have felt unable, unworthy, or not capable to work at or in the profession of our dreams.

As much as I would like everyone to be employed in the work of their dreams, I am also a realist. Family demands and the necessity of earning a living are going to impede even the most determined when it comes to changing their lives and direction. Integrating some of this into your life will allow you to test the waters, and at least be somewhat involved until more permanent changes can be made. As an example, if you've always wanted to act or be involved in producing a play, join the local little theater in your community. Every industry needs accountants and administrative staff. If you are in one of these fields, you can do the same work, usually for the same pay in a field, or with a firm more closely aligned with your overall interests or values. Volunteer.

It is often a long road before we feel that we achieve true financial empowerment. Unfortunately, in holding ourselves back, we may have been our own worst enemies, and inadvertently had the support of well meaning family members and friends. It is never too late to make changes in our lives to further our financial well-being, and to live a less stressful life in line with our values. Allow yourself to become fully empowered personally and financially.

Recommended Reading

The Courage to be Rich by Suze Orman

The Laws of Money Guidebook by Suze Orman

The Secret by Rhonda Byrne

Secrets of Six-Figure Women: Surprising Strategies to Up Your Earnings and

Change Your Life by Barbara Stanny

The Seven Habits of Highly Effective People by Dr. Steven Covey

Notes:

ABOUT THE AUTHOR

VERA MORGAN BYRD

Ms. Vera Morgan Byrd is President and CEO of Professional Resource, a professional development consulting and training firm, specializing in Customer Service, Leadership and Professional Development. Professional Resource offers educational, practical, inspirational, and professional guidance to its clients. Its workshops and seminars are filled with energy, enthusiasm, passion, and inspiration; and are geared to meet the client's needs while motivating the client to 'take action' as well as 'think outside the box.'

Ms. Byrd is a certified consultant and has been appointed to the Professional Woman Network Board of Directors. Ms. Byrd has over 27 years experience in the corporate environment (customer service, sales, marketing, public speaking, energy management, quality improvement, and human resources).

Ms. Byrd holds a bachelor degree in Business Management and has had involvement in Life Style Management, Image and Self-Projection, Effective Communication, Personnel Law, and Leadership and Supervisory Skills for Women.

Ms. Byrd has served on The Women Advisory Board – Plantation General Hospital (Broward County), Salvation Army Advisory Board – Lake Worth, Sickle Cell Foundation – Palm Beach County, Loan Executive to United Way – Palm Beach County, American Business Women Association – West Palm Beach, and is currently active with Hurst Chapel A.M.E. Church, Sigma Lamp of Learning Foundation, Gamma Gamma Sigma Chapter of Sigma Gamma Rho Sorority. Ms. Byrd is available to speak, consult and train on a local, regional and national basis.

Contact
Professional Resource
P.O. Box 221482
West Palm Beach, FL 33422-1482
(561) 307-5239
VeraDByrd@aol.com
www.protrain.net

NINETEEN

MEDIA INTERVIEWS: TIPS FOR TELEVISION AND RADIO

By Vera Byrd

"A good interview should have the character of a good novel."
—Harrison Salisbury

Say what you mean, mean what you say; the facts, just the facts; tell the truth, nothing but the whole truth. I'm quite sure we're familiar with these sayings. Interviewing is seeking answers, or looking for information by asking questions of another person.

Interviews can be one-on-one, group, and roundtable. You have print interviews, radio interviews and television interviews. In print interviews, you can introduce complicated things. The most in-depth interviews usually appear in print. With radio interviews, you can capture emotional content. And a television interview can be edited if it's not live.

All interviews require editing.

"The media is a powerful instrument that all too often goes unused."
—Lawrence Grobel, **The Art of the Interview.**

"We all recognize the power of the media. But all too often, people don't recognize that they too have some power when dealing with the media."
—Dennis Stauffer,
MediaSmart – How To Handle A Reporter, By A Reporter.

As an interviewee, you have something an interviewer wants. Only you can determine what you will provide. In providing information, always assume you're on the record, know what you can't say, and always be honest. You have the ability to choose what you say, and what you say is controlled by you.

To get your story told, you need to find a way to sell it. Now, you need to meet the need of the interviewer. Discover what interests you and the interviewer have in common, and use it to be heard. When you understand what the interviewer needs, and provide it, you can improve your chances of getting the interview.

You should know if you're an important element in an interview. Will the interview be about something you did, about your family, your business, about you, or an organization you're involved in? Don't be afraid to offer alternative arrangements for the interview if the suggested ones do not meet your approval. You want to be comfortable during your interview. For clarity, ask questions.

- What will be asked?

- Where will the interview take place?

- Time factors?

- Deadlines?

- How long will the interview take?

- Live or Taped?

- Show and Tell?

- Set reasonable limits.

You want to be able to handle the interview with ease. Once the interview is granted, be sure to ask when it will air and request a copy. According to Lawrence Grobel, "*Almost all interviews done these days in any medium are recorded, for the simple reason that the technology exists and legal departments demand accuracy.*"

Preparing for an interview can vary; it depends on who you are preparing for. And know that not all interviewers are sensitive to your cause. Just as the interviewer is prepared, the interviewee should also be prepared. In your interview, you want to let the interviewer know who you are. Remember, what you put into an interview is what you will get out of it. In an interview you want to:

- Dress well.

- Be patience.

- Be prepared.

- Be educated.

- Be current.

- Be natural.

- Know when to be forceful.

- Rely on your personality.

Make sure you are an active participant in the interview; this is not the time to be passive.

Make sure the interviewer has all the information needed to draw the conclusion you want. The interview is only as good as the information given. Garbage in, garbage out.

Keep in mind what audience you want to reach and select your media accordingly. Your interview may suit itself more to one media form than another. To quickly reach as many people as possible, you want television. Television is good at capturing emotions, problems, and large events such as Presidential debates and sporting events. When the interview requires a great deal of time and offers very little visuals, radio is your best media form. Radio allows for detailed answers, it's live, and gets the information out quickly.

During your interview, speak in the first person. You want to attract and hold your audience's attention, and you can do this by relating things in personal terms with good dialogue. Be sure to emphasize the significance of the interview. Be outspoken. But again remember, nothing is off the record. Make sure you give facts that will uphold your view or cause. Stress key points. Explain yourself, give details and make your case. Use humor and analogies, but avoid clichés, jargons, and technical terms pertaining to your profession. Be sure to look at the interviewer and not the camera. Don't ramble to fill time. Keep track of when the camera is rolling. If you feel you have misspoken, ask to re-state what was said. Don't be defensive and uncertain; being credible is important. Feel free to record the interview yourself. It can serve the following purposes:

- Method to review your performance

- Your record of the interview

- Keeps interviewer honest

- Prevents misquotes

It's a good idea to leave relevant information with the interviewer in the form of a press packet, as well.

I have done several television and radio interviews; I must say I was quite nervous each time I did them. Knowing your subject matter is a plus, but practicing also helps. Pull out the video camera and record yourself. Now, evaluate your performance.

Are you articulating well? Do you have any nervous tics? Are you pronouncing your words clearly? Are you speaking too fast? How is your posture? Do practice to hone your interview skills.

To get a professional's point of view on interviewing, I had the privilege of interviewing a local television reporter, Ms. Angela Rozier.

Q: How long should an interview last?
Angela: As long as it takes to get the information you need.

Q: Should the interviewer and interviewee agree on what
            questions to be asked?

Angela: No. I don't know what I want to ask. I may get another
            question from an answer given.

Q: What do you do when an interview has gone bad or is
            going bad?

Angela: I try not to ask yes/no questions. I ask questions that need to
            be expound upon.

Q: What type questions are off base in an interview?

Angela: It depends on the story. I stay on the subject.

Q: During an interview, is it okay to use notes?

Angela: Sure, no problem. Anything to make the interviewee
            comfortable.

Q: What determines a successful interview?

Angela: To get someone to open up and tell me things they might
            not have told someone else.

Q: When does an interview infringe on the privacy of the
            interviewee?

Angela: When the interviewee denies your request time and time
            again and yet you continue to harass him/her.

Q: Is it ever okay for the interviewee to bring a guest into
            the interview?

Angela: The more the better. It makes me, the interviewer, more comfortable. Now I can get information from the both of them.

Q: What do you think is the difference between a television and radio interview?

Angela: Just the picture. People are more intimidated with the camera. Usually, radio and print has more time.

Q: What tips would you give an interviewee?

Angela: Be relaxed. Don't say anything you don't want anyone to know.

Again, what you put into an interview is what you will get out of it.

Therefore, remember how you look is almost as important as what is said. So, relax, be prepared, rely on your personality, and make sure you are an active participant in the interview.

Reading References

The Art of the Interview by Lawrence Grobel

MediaSmart – How to Handle A Reporter (By A Reporter) by Dennis Stauffer

ABOUT THE AUTHOR

Ruby M. Ashley, MBA

Ruby Ashley is Chief Executive Officer of Ruby Ashley & Associates. She is a leader in personal and professional development, specializing in the delivery of workshops, seminars, training programs, and assessments. Her workshops and training programs are highly interactive and stimulating with focus on improving employee performance. She firmly believes that as long as individuals are willing to learn, change, and grow, they will always reach high levels of achievement.

Ms. Ashley is an accomplished motivational keynote speaker, facilitator, trainer, and consultant with more than 26 years of experience in the corporate environment. As a Certified Customer Service Trainer, she delivers an outstanding Customer Service Excellence program. Other training program topics include: personal and professional development, women's issues, diversity and multiculturalism, self-esteem, leadership development, strategic planning, road map to retirement, and team building. Teen topics are Save Our Youth, Teen Image, and Leadership.

Ms. Ashley earned Bachelor's and Master's degrees in Business from Brenau University in Gainesville, GA. She is a member of The Professional Woman Network (PWN), is a certified trainer, and member of The PWN International Advisory Board. Ms. Ashley holds memberships in other professional organizations, including the American Business Woman Association, Toastmasters International, Les Brown Speaker's Bureau, and is an affiliate of Leadership Development Group, Inc. She is a youth mentor and an active volunteer in her community.

Ruby Ashley is also a co-author of *Becoming the Professional Woman, Self-Esteem & Empowerment for Women* and *The Young Woman's Guide for Personal Success* in the PWN Library.

Contact
Ruby Ashley & Associates
1735 Chatham Ridge Circle #206
Charlotte, NC 28273
(404) 316-5931
rbyash@aol.com
www.protrain.net

TWENTY

WOMEN IN LEADERSHIP: ESSENTIAL SKILLS FOR SUCCESS

By Ruby Ashley

Leadership in the 21st Century
Gone are the days of managers limiting the information they share with employees on a simple "need to know" basis. Smart leaders are no longer using a "hands off" style of management or a "this is my team" concept. As a leader, you are now expected to include employees in all your phases of planning, including setting goals and the final decision-making process. Today's leaders must take on new roles not expected of them in the past. Leaders are now seen as facilitators of self-directed teams. In fact, in order for any leader to be successful,

she must be willing to acquire and execute some basic core skills and qualities that will be necessary for their success.

QUALITIES A LEADER NEEDS INCLUDE BEING:		
✓ Confident	✓ Dedicated	✓ Approachable
✓ Realistic	✓ Influential	✓ Committed
✓ Positive	✓ Willing	✓ Truthful
✓ Resourceful	✓ Flexible	✓ Organized
✓ Knowledgeable	✓ Cooperative	✓ Reliable

SKILLS A LEADER NEEDS INCLUDE:
✓ Creating Value
✓ Finding Solutions
✓ Accurately Assessing Situations

In order to determine your potential as a good leader, it is important to take the time to *continuously* assess your skills and qualities. You should also honestly evaluate your capability to change, because your flexibility will ensure not only your personal growth, but also your future success. After a self-assessment review of the areas you can develop and improve, it's time to create a plan of action.

Leadership Self-Assessment

On the lines below, write how you would define the word leadership.

_____

_____

Do You Recognize Your Leadership Abilities?

	From the list of words below, choose the five that represent your strongest leadership qualities and place an "S" beside them. Then choose the five that represent your weakest leadership characteristics and write a "W" beside them. After you have placed the letters beside the words, then number them from 1 to 5 with "1S" representing your strongest trait and "1W" representing your weakest trait.		
	Communicating		Counseling
	Mentoring		Creating Innovative Solutions
	Coaching		Problem-Solving
	Training		Goal-Setting
	Delegating		Influencing Others

Some of the questions you should ask yourself when considering whether you should take on a leadership role are:

1) Am I ready for leadership?

2) Do I like to learn and share information?

3) Do I enjoy motivating and leading others?

4) Am I capable of building a high performance team?

5) Can I help others succeed?

There will always be areas that you will be stronger in than others; however, you can, with determination and dedication, develop in those areas where you are weak and lacking.

Once you have identified your five weak areas from the prior list, take the ones you labeled "1W" and write a plan of action to become stronger in that area. You can, with continued self-improvement and self-assessment, become a successful leader.

> *"I'll tell you what leadership is.*
> *It's persuasion, and conciliation and education and patience."*
> —Dwight D. Eisenhower

Successful Leadership Skills

Both the ability to influence others and the amount of personal power someone has contributes to that person's success as a leader. Many people mistakenly believe that men have an advantage over women when it comes to these qualities. However, women in leadership today are developing their personal power along with their ability to persuade others, in order to become better leaders. While there may be some similarities between the leadership styles among different women, most will perform their leadership roles in a unique manner that is different from everyone else. Because there are dozens of skills, traits, and qualities that experts view as "must haves" for leaders at various companies and organizations, each person's personality and character traits will be the determining factor in whether or not a particular individual succeeds as a leader in that particular corporate culture.

Character Values

> *"Leadership is a potent combination of strategy and character.*
> *But if you must be without one, be without strategy."*
> **—Norman Schwarzkopt**

Your character is number one. A leader of character brings honesty, ethics, and authenticity to the workplace. There will be occasions when you and an employee will not agree. If it turns out that a particular incident leaves you and someone else at odds with each other and you decide to discuss it with your manager, you must be truthful and honest about what happened. In other words, don't make yourself look good at the other person's expense. You don't want to take the easy way out by leaving out important information, and therefore, placing fault and blame on the employee. Why? You don't want to put that person's job in jeopardy.

Many managers will not ask the employee for his/her side of the story and will take what you say to be truthful. Unfortunately, there are many people who would rather be right than fair. And in my opinion, many leaders fail in this area because they are too concerned with making themselves look good. It is not about looking good when someone else's future is on the line. It is about doing and saying what is right. If a mistake was made, make sure there is some "knowledge learned from the mistake," that would prevent it from happening again. Then it will be "a lesson well-learned." It's impossible to do any job without making mistakes, so give yourself and others a break. Realize that we're all human, and it is important to treat others the same way you would expect to be treated. **Being a real leader means facing the music, even when you dislike the tune.**

Professional Image

Another essential component to becoming a good leader is maintaining your professional image. A professional image includes the kind of clothes you wear, your body language, your voice, posture, poise, and self-confidence. You, the leader, are responsible for adhering to the company's dress policy and should, at all times, wear clothing that is appropriate. Depending on the company and type of work you do, dress codes will vary from business formal to business casual or just casual. The dress code over the last ten years has changed dramatically. Now, many companies are going back to business formal attire. The reason for this change is because they have found that employees who are allowed to wear more casual attire seem to be less productive.

Some leaders have the self-confidence that they need to be effective in their position, but lack the ability to express themselves effectively through their body language. Did you know that body language expresses 55 percent of any message you want to convey? Using ineffective body language may give those around you the wrong message. Ask yourself this question: When holding a conversation or meeting with someone, do you look at this person directly in the eyes, or do you avoid eye contact? In a business setting, it is important to always hold your head up and give your full attention to the person talking to you.

Did you know that about 38 percent of the meaning you convey to others is dependent on your voice communication? For example, many people interpret leaders who have soft-spoken voices to also have a meek and passive character. However, I've seen someone in a leadership position use her soft voice to her advantage, actually getting what she wanted because of her approach. In general, though, it is best to speak in a way that makes your voice seem appropriately loud, strong, firm, relaxed, and well-modulated.

Your character and self-image ultimately denote who you are. How you walk, what you say, how you say it, and what you wear all represent you, and create not only a professional image, but also a level of personal assertiveness that will determine your effectiveness as leader.

People Skills

Having the necessary people skills is crucial to the success of any leader. Some of these people skills include: effective communication, as well as empowering and motivating others.

Along with being an essential leadership tool, effective communication also tops the list of people skills. Your ability to communicate with others will be necessary for your success. The old cliché, "It's not what you say, but how you say it," is still true today. When discussing your game plan, don't ever assume that some things are understood without explanation. You must have the ability to communicate your vision and ideas so everyone can understand clearly what you are saying.

Be open and listen to what others have to say. Should you find yourself in a situation where you feel uncomfortable, or where someone asks you a question and you don't have the answer, tell that person you will find out and get back with them. Be approachable, so others will want to communicate with you when they have a problem or concern. You will always want to keep the lines of communication open within your group.

Empowering others is another important skill. As a leader, you are responsible for equipping employees with the tools they need to perform their jobs. You will have to provide information and encourage others to participate in the decision-making process. Getting involved helps give individuals a sense of self-worth, and makes them feel like their input is valued, thus boosting their morale. Don't feel threatened or stifle someone's idea if it is better than yours. Be enthusiastic and show your appreciation. You may be surprised to find that their specific job role within the company gives them a unique, detailed perspective, which will allow them to provide useful recommendations that may result in improved performance for everyone.

Motivation is yet another essential people skill, which varies from person to person. What motivates one employee may not motivate another; so you, the leader, will need to know your employees' hot buttons and how best to motivate each one individually. While it's true that motivation can only come from within a person, it's a leader's job to obtain knowledge of his/her employee's individual personalities, and capitalize on them by taking specific actions that will encourage each person to perform to his/her highest capability.

For some employees, tangibles such as bonuses, pension plans, travel allowances, paid education, medical plans, and job security motivate them; while for others, the intangibles of praise, job challenges, and job satisfaction are enough. You, as a leader, should be able to recognize what best motivates your employee, whether it be achievement, recognition, responsibility, advancement, or growth. One form of motivation I used when I was in a leadership position was to recognize excellent performance by placing stars on employees' daily reports. This was something each employee waited for with anticipation because it meant they excelled in all the areas shown on their report; and of course, if they excelled, the team excelled. Besides motivating your employees, it is just as important to motivate yourself. You, yourself, must be motivated to do a good job and to succeed because your employees will be able to tell if you are genuine or just giving the minimum effort required to get the job done.

Team Development / Building

Developing or building your team will first require you to have a vision or goals. This will be followed closely by you getting to know your employees' roles, and being committed to their success, as well as the success of the team. When Helen Keller was asked, "What would be worse than being born blind?" she replied, "To have sight without vision." You have to know where you are going, and more importantly, you will need your team's help and participation. It's important to write down your goals, so you can communicate them effectively at any given time. Also, make sure your team takes ownership, making your vision their vision.

You will be responsible for getting to know your team members and taking the time to discover their unique abilities. Spend time interviewing each team member, asking them direct questions like: what do you enjoy about your job? What do you dislike about it? Carefully review their past performance, and take note of the areas where they need improvement. Write a plan and share it with them, giving them on-going progress reports. Emphasize the importance of their performance, and remind them that they will be rewarded according to the extent of their contribution.

Also, keep reminding them of your vision or goal. I actually followed this process and was able to help employees increase their performance, thereby increasing the team's performance. I wholeheartedly support and believe in the team concept that "Together Everyone Achieves More." I made a concerted effort to be accessible and approachable to everyone. It took a while, but after recognizing the importance of letting go and delegating job duties to employees, more time was spent focusing on other issues, such as job performance. Being approachable gives your employees the leeway to discuss difficult personal situations that you need to be aware of. It also gives them the freedom to make recommendations and voice their opinions or concerns. Being approachable is a powerful concept that promotes confidence, trust, and support. It's also very important to always give employees timely feedback in the form of coaching and training. Always be willing to give team members recognition for a job well done, and reassure them that they have a voice.

Resolving Conflict Resolution

Conflict Resolution is not about being nice, liked, or popular. Instead, it's about being able to mediate disputes effectively. Effective dispute resolution skills will gain you respect from others. So, when there is conflict, leaders must step up and deal with it directly, never being afraid to use their authority and power to resolve the issue. Warning! Don't prejudge the other party. If you do, it sets the tone for negativity. Give the person involved an opportunity to share his/her side of what's going on. It is very important to keep a positive attitude when dealing with a conflict in order to ensure you are not using your authority in the wrong way. If you handle the situation poorly, you could create an even greater problem that will result in decreased performance, morale problems, and poor decision-making. However, if handled properly, this same conflict could result in increased production, better motivation, and the added ability to make good decisions.

You should be aware that, if you are tempted to use the word "problem" when dealing with a conflict, you should replace it with the word "challenge", since it will be less likely to have a negative connotation to the person hearing it. Also, as much as possible, you should include the words "opportunity," "growth," and "innovation." These three words, combined with your positive motivation, should inspire you to make an extra effort to resolve any difficulty you encounter.

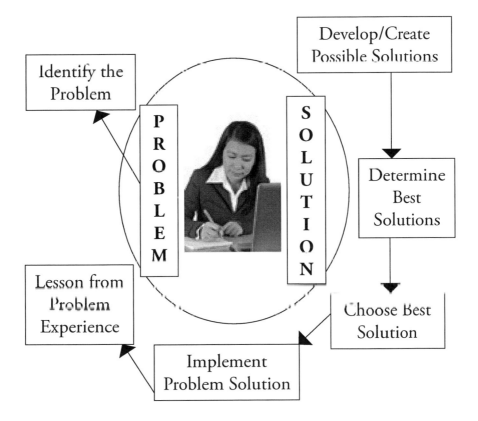

Conclusion

The book, *More Than A Pink Cadillac: Mary Kay Inc.'s 9 Leadership Keys To Success* by Jim Underwood is a story about an awesome woman who made a $5,000.00 investment into her dream, and now the company is doing billions of dollars in wholesale sales worldwide. Mary Kay learned early about the importance of leadership skills and what she calls the "positive power of Great!" Because of her positive attitude, people around her became more positive, more enthusiastic, and their performance soared. As a leader, your positive attitude will be an important part of your success. So will your ability to motivate, inspire, and challenge others to do what they think they cannot do. Should you aspire to be a leader, don't be afraid. Prepare yourself by gaining experience and knowledge through reading books, attending conferences, watching other leaders, and seeking a mentor. Never become complacent with your skill level and knowledge. Be determined and committed to a course of continuous learning and the acquisition of knowledge.

The following is a quote from a speech given by Mary Kay Ash to her sales force leaders:

"We need leaders who add value to the people and the organization they lead; for the benefit of others and not just for their own personal gain; who inspire and motivate rather than intimidate and manipulate; who live with people to know their problems, and live with God in order to solve them; and who follow a moral compass that points in the right direction, regardless of the trends."

I dedicate this chapter to all the women currently holding leadership roles, as well as those who aspire to become leaders sometime in the future.

Suggested Readings:

The Twelve Universal Laws of Success by Herbert Harris

Developing the Leader Within You by John C. Maxwell

CareerPreneurs Lessons From Leading Women Entrepreneurs: On Building A Career Without Boundaries by Dorothy Perrin Moore

More Than A Pink Cadillac: Mary Kay Inc.'s 9 Leadership Keys to Success by Jim Underwood

ABOUT THE AUTHOR

DAPHNE C. FERGUSON-YOUNG, DDS, MSPH

Dr. Ferguson-Young received her DDS degree and MSPH degree from Meharry Medical College. She also completed a General Practice Residency certificate program at Meharry Medical College.

Most of Dr. Ferguson-Young's professional career has been dedicated to working with individuals who have limited access to healthcare. She worked for over thirteen years at Matthew Walker Community Health Center. Dr. Ferguson-Young was in private practice before accepting a faculty appointment at Meharry Medical College, School of Dentistry. She also is a contract dentist with the Indian Health Service where she has had the opportunity to provide dental services to the Sioux Tribe in North Dakota. Dr. Ferguson-Young also serves in the USAR as a Major and was deployed to Iraq in 2004. Her tour of duty gave her the opportunity to provide dental services to Iranian detainees as well as to the American servicemen and servicewomen.

Dr. Ferguson-Young is currently an Assistant Professor in the Department of Restorative Dentistry where she teaches 2nd, 3rd, and 4th year dental students both pre clinically and clinically.

She is very active in several dental professional, academic, and community activities where she serves in several leadership capacities. Dr. Ferguson-Young is active with Capital City Dental Society, PanTN Dental Association and the National Dental Association. She currently is a member of the Mathew Walker Community Health Center Governing Board. Recently, she was selected to participate in the first National Dental Society-Glaxo Smith Kline Speakers' Bureau.

Dr, Ferguson-Young has presented several professional presentations on the local, state, national and international level. She has been the recipient of several teaching awards.

Dr. Daphne C. Ferguson-Young continues to dedicate her professional life as an advocate and activist for access to quality healthcare for all individuals.

Contact
Dr. Daphne C. Ferguson-Young
2120 Lebanon Pike #38
Nashville, TN 37210
(615) 889-7760
dajayou@bellsouth.net

TWENTY-ONE

COMMUNICATION: WHAT'S THE DIFFERENCE?

By Daphne Young

"I understand a fury in your words, but not the words."
—William Shakespeare

How many times have you been engaged in a "simple" conversation with a male colleague, husband, or brother only to suddenly feel like you are speaking a foreign language? Well, the fact is…..as a woman, you **are** speaking a different language!!

There is evidence to show that a communication gap definitely exists between men and women. But a communication gap also exists between more than just the genders. We will explore in this chapter that there are different ways of presenting and listening, and that female leaders may also have their message fall onto "deaf ears" of female listeners, as well.

You are familiar with the saying, "I know you think that you understand what I said, but I'm not sure that what you heard is what I meant." Let's begin by looking at if this may be true.

There really is a reason that we have TWO ears and ONE mouth! Hearing with an open mind is critical to interpersonal communication, but sometimes men, in particular, may seem to be absorbed in some other project as they nod their heads, as if to be listening. That may hurt your feelings, but it is true that men and women have very different communication styles. Let's take a look at facts.

First of all, the verbal part of communicating is only 7%, while the nonverbal part is 93%. One hears the words, but is also interpreting facial expressions, the tone of the message, and the position of the body. So in essence, the message that one is attempting to convey may easily be misinterpreted, due to body language clouding over the meaning, and resulting in being misunderstood.

So, where do we start in learning how to communicate effectively? First, we have to start with ourselves. The more that we know and understand about ourselves and our personalities, the easier it will be for us to be effective. It is important that we have a grasp of our particular behavior style. A behavioral style indicates our values and comfort zone.

There are personality tests available to determine one's particular area. By understanding our behavioral style, we understand and accept not only our strengths, but also our weaknesses. We have a more intimate knowledge of our reaction and interaction with other behavioral styles. One system of behavioral styles is the Social Model. The four dimensions are the following: analytical, driving, amiable and expressive. The model will give one a better overview of each.

Dealing With Emotions			
A S K S	Analytical Controls emotions, voice usually monotone, more reserved, focuses on facts and data Orientation: Thinking	Driving Controls emotions, but more vocal, speaks directly and loudly, focuses on results and outcomes Orientation: Action	T E L L S
	Amiable Displays emotions, speaks slowly, concerned with relationships Orientation: Relationships	Expressive Displays emotions, talks more and faster, not monotone, highly spontaneous Orientation: Future	
Displays Emotions			

Exercise

1. 1.Who are you? Take a look at the previous chart and consider if you are Analytical, Driving, Expressive, or Amiable. Place your name in the box.

2. List people in your life (co-workers, family, friends) and type of "Social Model" they are.

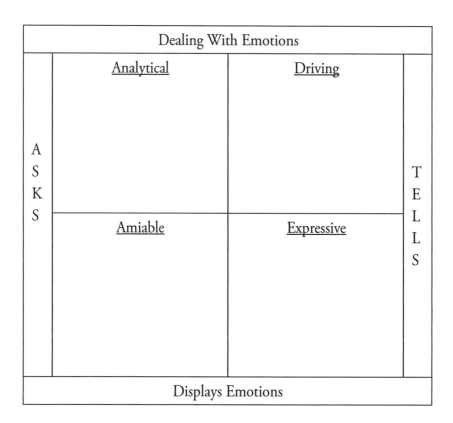

3. Consider these people, and now make a note on the previous chart as
    to problem relationships that have occurred because of communication
    misunderstanding between "Social Model" styles. List names.

4. How could you alter your "communication style" to be able to better
    communicate with certain "problem" people? (i.e. be more direct, listen
    more, speak more assertively, etc.)

Person #1: _____

Person #2: _____

Person #3: _____

Along with understanding the Social Model, we should also be familiar with the Verbal Model and verbal patterns of communication. Just as individuals are visual, auditory, and kinesthetic or touching learners, we also tend communicate this way. For instance, the **visual communicator** focuses on images and uses statements such as, "Give me the big picture", or "Look at it from my viewpoint". The **auditory** communicator uses reason and logic with such statements as, "That sounds good", or "Just give me the facts." The **kinesthetic** communicator focuses on experience and intuition. They use statements such as, "I don't have a good feeling about that", or "Let's stay in touch about that."

By having a working understanding of one's communications style from The Social Model and Verbal Model, we can begin to communicate with others within their comfort zone, as well as yours.

Exercise
Looking at The Verbal Model chart, list your name under a specific communication style, and also friends, colleagues, and family members.

Visual	Auditory	Kinesthetic

Are you able to adjust your speaking to incorporate some of their "communication styles" when you communicate with them?

There are barriers that we face everyday, which complicates communication. Some of these barriers are the following:

1. **Different perceptions**: based upon how we selected and organized the information we have received and interpreted to fit our desires

2. **External distractions**: noise, weather, nearby conversations, music, lights, traffic noise

3. **Intentions**: misinterpreting one's actions based upon our perception

4. **Nonverbal communications**: ignoring the nonverbal signals, which are apparent when someone is communicating with us

At times, it's the nonverbal that may keep you from being taken seriously, or even just being heard...period! What are some of the nonverbal pieces? Let's start with *appearance*. A first impression is a lasting impression! What is your style of clothing saying about you? Is your style professional, playful, flirty? Does the style fit you, your personality, the setting (work, conference, vacation, job interview) and the occasion? How about the makeup, the hair, and the shoes?

There is a saying that says, "Dress for the position you want, not the one you have." What type of facial expressions do you "wear" daily? Do you frown a lot or do you appear joyful and happy? Do your words mirror your expressions?

What about body language? Do you look down, as if lacking confidence? Do you invade others' personal space? Are your hand gestures and movements appropriate for the conversation? What about your voice? How is the volume? Do people have to constantly ask you to speak up? Do you speak slowly with emphasis in different places in order to make your point? Having an image of how you look conversing with others can be quite insightful. Practice in front of the mirror before doing a presentation. Invest in a tape recorder to become comfortable with your voice. Ask a close friend for an honest evaluation of how you present yourself to others.

Remember, it is not so much what you say, it is the way you say it. Constantly remind yourself that the very way you deliver information to another human being is predicated in large part on the way you say it, and how you appear while you say it!

Listening

But what about that other very important aspect of communicating? Listening.......

How do we become effective listeners? First, we have to understand the process of listening. The process involves the following:

1. **Receiving** the spoken word from the speaker

2. **Interpreting** the message so that it makes sense

3. **Responding** in a manner that lets the speaker know that you understood

There are different types of listeners. They are:

1. **The Passive Listener**: This individual doesn't show any emotions on their face; they may or may not have good eye contact; they alternate between nodding and sitting with no expression on their face; it is difficult to really understand if they are listing at all.

2. **The Selective Listener**: This individual is easily distracted; may interrupt to take over the conversation; likes to change subjects.

3. **The Active Listener**: This individual stays focused on what someone is saying; they avoid listening barriers such as distractions; may tend to "lean into" the speaker; excellent eye contact; nods head to communicate understanding.

Researchers have discovered that only 50% of information is retained immediately after hearing a speech. The retention decreases drastically as the hours pass by. In order to be an effective listener, you will need to minimize any distractions and avoid or limit interruptions.

How effective are you as a communicator? Check the list and see what you can discover about yourself

Self-Evaluation of Effective Communication

	Sometimes	Always	Never
I don't listen to people who don't share my point of view.			
I find it easy to listen to people with different viewpoints.			
I make eye contact with the speaker.			
I feel that I can communicate my viewpoint comfortably with anybody.			
I try to consider how I can best communicate with others.			
I do not become defensive when I am given negative feedback.			
I become easily distracted when someone is talking to me.			
I repeat information back to make sure that I understand.			
I practice my listening skills every day so that I can become an effective communicator.			

As a woman who is currently in a leadership position (or wishing to attain the role of a leader), constantly reflect on the message you are presenting to others. Consider the listening style of the other person. Could you consider telling a short story to prove your point? How might you dress for this specific meeting so that you message is taken seriously? Also, keep in mind the importance of listening (rather than simply *hearing)* closely to what others say, and always keep distractions to a minimum. Avoid having your own "agenda" or a ready-answer when listening. Be open to changing your mind.

Every person communicates differently, but it is the wise leader who knows her team and herself. By searching within and understanding your verbal and listening styles, you will be able to better understand the differences in others. Be on your toes at all times, and learn to adapt to other's styles so that you message (and theirs) will be more easily understood.

I wish you success with closing the Communication Gap that exists between many people. Teach others to "be on the same page" with those that they are communicating with. Communication is a process, and the speaker and listener are both responsible for being certain that the message is not lost.

Recommended Reading

How to Speak and Listen Effectively by Harvey A. Robbins

The Secret Language of Success by David Lewis

Talking Power by Robin Tolmach Lakoff

Notes:

ABOUT THE AUTHOR

KIMBERLY ARMSTRONG

Kimberly Armstrong is the President of Diamond Development Inc. a Consulting & Training organization which provides services to families, professionals and community-involved individuals on stress & anger management, building self-esteem, leadership, diversity and other life enhancement skills. She has completed trainings and received certificates from The Professional Woman Network, and the Women's Entrepreneurs of Baltimore (W.E.B).

Her advocacy about youth violence has lead her to become a sought-after speaker and commentator, and she has appeared in many venues including the Marc Steiner Radio Show, the Baltimore Sun, Washington Post, and University of Maryland Capitol News, as well as at Maryland's Juvenile Justice Coalition's Monthly Speakers Forum, the Women's Entrepreneurs of Baltimore's Work Force Development Workshop, and the

Maryland State Assembly her personal testimonial for legislated bills to helped reform the Maryland Juvenile System, she has been the guest and key note speaker, the latest being the guest speaker for the National Cease-Fire Against Gun Violence in Nashville, Tennessee.

Ms. Armstrong suffered a tragic loss in September 2004 when her young son was murdered; this has lead her to embark on another journey as an Author, She is one of 25 women who co-authored *The Christians Woman's Guide For Personal Succes,* her chapter being *"How to deal with death and grief."*

Kimberly thrives on and believes that the best way to help others is to help them find the Brilliance in helping themselves.

In December 2004 she received the 2004-2005 Pollin Award from the Washington Wizards for Outstanding Dedication to the Community, and in 2007 she was Honored by the National Juvenile Justice Network and the Campaign for Youth Justice with The National Mother of Distinction Award. These accomplishments have made her an ardent proponent for positive, constructive and immediate reform of the entire juvenile justice system in Maryland. She continues to fight injustice and helps youth & families help themselves through education and empowerment.

Ms. Armstrong is the former Interim Co-Chair for the Maryland Juvenile Justice Coalition, and Founder/Executive Director of the Just 4 Me Mentoring Program for Girls. Ms. Armstrong is currently a board member for the Governor's Office of Crime Control and Prevention (GOCCP) and The Juvenile Detention Alternative Initiative (JDAI) with the Annie E. Casey Foundation and the Department of Juvenile Services in Baltimore Maryland where she resides..

Contact
Founder & Director
Diamond Development Inc. & Just 4 Me Mentoring Program for Girls
(410)483-5998
Just4Me .Diamond@gmail.com
www.DiamondDevelopmentinc.net
www.pwnbooks.com

TWENTY-TWO

LEADERSHIP SKILLS FOR YOUTH

By Kimberly Armstrong

This chapter is written for you, the young woman who aspires to become a leader.

Who are you? Knowing who you are is the first step and the key to becoming an effective leader. Growing and developing is a process that all humans must go through in stages.

The stages are: birth, infant, toddler; then we gradually began to move up into childhood and begin to consider what life is all about. We start to explore in several areas, such as talking, discovering new words, observing people, places and the things around us. All of these will contribute to who you are (and will be) some day.

I know as a young person or a youth that you may not truly understand or realize it now, but when you reach my age of 30 something, (yes, you may say "THAT'S OLD") you will begin to look back and remember events in your youth that contributed to your becoming a great leader.

What is Leadership?

Many leadership theorists currently agree that leaders are made, not born. And that young people can learn and develop leadership attitudes and skills outlined in five areas of competency that distinguish leaders and shape youth leadership development efforts:

• **Communication** – persuasive argumentation, public speaking/writing, and engaging the participation of others. List courses you are taking or activities you are involved in currently: (i.e. drama, debate, etc)

1. _____

2. _____

• **Teamwork** – respecting others, performing roles of both leader and follower, building on strengths, and commitment to free group input and expression;

In what way are you currently on a team? (i.e. band, church choir, soccer)

1. _____

2. _____

• **Personal Identity** – understanding the relationship between oneself and the community, pride in being a member of a larger group, awareness of areas for self-improvement, taking responsibility for one's actions and the resulting consequences. What are you doing to help your community? (i.e. volunteering)

1. _____

2. _____

• **Professionalism** – demonstrating tactfulness, understanding protocols, appropriate dress and action given appraisal of context, delivering quality work, positively presenting oneself to others. If you work currently, in what way do you present yourself professionally?

1. _____

2. _____

• **Project Management** – setting goals/developing action steps, meeting facilitation, reflection. On what projects (at school or work) are you currently working? Have you set goals for each?

1. _____

2. _____

Becoming a leader is a developmental process, and this process may not be the same for young people as it is for adults. Young people need to develop their leadership skills in "real situations" that they deem important, which allows them to become actively engaged "in the decision-making processes" affecting their lives. Begin to ask yourself some serious questions about leadership to see if you are equipped, committed, and have the passion to lead. Remember that others will be watching and depending on you for instruction and guidance. Accountability, responsibility, and the ability to persuade others to change or to make a difference is what being an EFFECTIVE LEADER is all about.

Why Is It Important For Young People to Develop Leadership?

Many leadership scholars and youth development professionals agree that leadership development is an important, but often overlooked facet of youth development and education. **Adults can many times hinder youth from becoming leaders by not allowing them to solve their own problems or creating solutions for change**.

The development of leadership contributes greatly to the positive development of young people and their communities. Leadership skills, such as goal-setting, problem-solving, and sound decision-making, are not just necessary for leaders. These skills are needed for success in today's world. Furthermore, helping young people develop leadership competencies makes them better able to solve community problems and enhances their civic participation. Young leaders also demonstrate higher career aspirations, increased self-esteem, and improved high school completion rates.

I hear this quote all the time, and I tend to *disagree* with the way adults use it, "Youth are our future of tomorrow." Yes, youth may leaders of tomorrow, but they can also be molded into leaders for *today!* Even though all young people will not become leaders of an organization or group, they most certainly will have to *lead their own lives.*

What Can Youth Professionals Do to Help Young People Develop Leadership Skills?

In developing leadership skills, young people face unique obstacles, some of which are posed by adults who (1) think leadership is something that one "grows into" or earns; (2) don't believe young people are capable of being leaders today; (3) are unwilling to share their power, responsibility, and decision-making, and (4) just assign young people to tasks, rather than allowing them to determine what happens in program planning, design, implementation, and evaluation. To overcome these obstacles and help young people effectively develop leadership skills, adult allies can:

1. Promote youth/adult partnerships, and give young people real power to make decisions and take responsibility for the consequences of their decisions.

2. Ensure that young people are provided with the training and support needed to take on new levels of responsibility and decision-making.

3. Provide a broad range of contexts, which allow young people to learn and develop leadership in the real world with diverse and unfamiliar groups.

4. Recognize and respect the knowledge, experience, and skills that young people have now, while still challenging them to enhance these skills and try new things.

Adults play a critical role in helping young people develop as leaders. Working with adults, young people can learn about the many different leaders and leadership styles, and the ways that leadership, and beliefs about leadership, are shaped by culture, values, and life experiences. Adults can support them to find or create the style that's right for themselves. Finally, adults can help dismantle the barriers that might prevent a young person from authentic engagement in leadership roles, and help create opportunities to learn and practice leadership in ways that make a real difference to them, their organizations, and their communities.

What Can Cause a Person to Become a Leader?

Issues and concerns cause a true leader to rise up and take a stand for change. After an issue has been clearly identified, leaders find committed people and bring them together to help find a solution to the issue. The solution then needs to be documented, shared, and replicated, so that others can help as well.

Exercise

What is a cause you are very passionate about? (i.e. Human Rights, Injustice, elder abuse, treatment of the mentally ill)

1. _____

What do you think can be done to help your cause?

1. _____

2. _____

3. _____

What are you prepared to do so that you can make a difference and become a leader in this area?

1. _____

2. _____

What personal traits do you possess that would make you an excellent leader?

1. _____

2. _____

Who is one person you know (or have read about) who is an exceptional leader? Why?

Person: _____

Traits:

1. _____

2. _____

3. _____

Developing a Plan of Action.

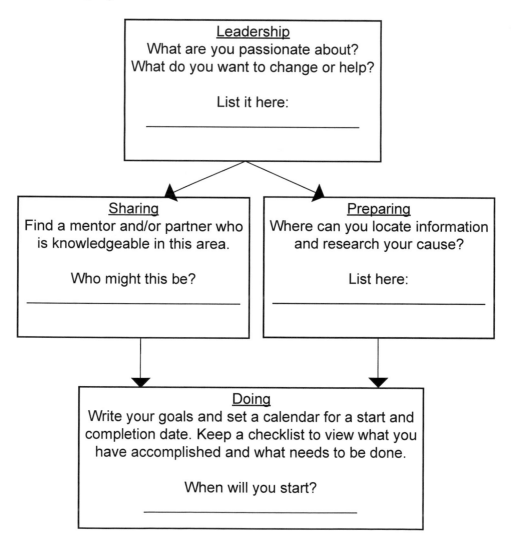

The internet is a great place to start. Here are some resources for your journey to becoming an Effective Leader I wish you much success and hope you enjoy the ride.

Youth Leadership Resources

www.NationWideSpeakers.com

www.SuperCamp.com

www.CampusBooks.com

www.smarter.com

www.DaleCarnegie.com

info@breakthroughcollaborative.org

http://www.atthetable.org

http://www.choosetolead.com/ataglance.htm

http://freechild.org/youth_leadership.htm

www.YouthSpeakCollective.org

http://www.theinnovationcenter.org/i_leader_dev.shtml

http://www.youthleadership.com

http://leadingtoday.org

www.urbanleadershipinstitute.org

www.urbanyouth.org

ABOUT THE AUTHOR

ELIZABETH M. WATERBURY, P.E., P.P., C.M.E.

Elizabeth Waterbury is the President and founder of E. M. Waterbury & Associates Consulting Engineers, a successful Consulting Engineering firm specializing in Land Use and Land Use Development. The focus of her career is to provide quality professional engineering services with a commitment to innovation and personal attention. Ms. Waterbury's firm consists of a talented group of female professionals and support staff who have made their mark in this specialized field of engineering, which is highly competitive and dominated by larger engineering firms.

When not working in her firm, Ms. Waterbury mentors others in professionalism, leadership and balance. This is accomplished through her many and diverse roles that vary from university professor to providing speeches as a member of The Professional Woman International Speakers Bureau. Her unique ability to channel her technical mind into creative and down-to-earth communication allows her to mentor to a broad range of individuals. One of her most honored rolls was to be the keynote speaker for the Southwest Regional Conference for the Society of Woman Engineer's. She has also been honored as a member of the International Advisory Board for The Professional Woman Network since 1990.

Her most cherished role is that of mother. She has worked hard since her daughter's birth to raise her daughter while running her firm. She is well versed in the difficulties that face women who wish to pursue their career, as well as be active in their family's lives. Her message of balance, defining personal success, and personal empowerment is carried through in all of her endeavors.

Contact
Elizabeth Waterbury, P.E., P.P., C.M.E.
E. M. Waterbury & Associates, P.A.
17 Monmouth Street
Red Bank, NJ 07701
(732) 747-6530
Fax (732) 747-6778
EMWAssoc@aol.com
www.protrain.net

TWENTY-THREE

CONFRONTING FEAR

By Elizabeth Waterbury

Over the past six years, I have had the experience of spending the last moments of life with seven significant family members. They have taught me quite a bit about facing fear.

Some passed after they have been through long illnesses. Some have passed quickly and unexpectedly. Some passed because their bodies failed. Some because their heart was broken and could not heal. It is the ultimate letting go and loss of control for both parties.

I found that the difficulty in spending moments with those that I loved was that it brought me face to face with my own mortality. I have had outsiders question me as to why I would be willing to place myself in that situation. It is emotional. It is unpredictable. I offer that there is an intimacy that I experienced with each and every one of these loved ones that, by going through their death with them, has helped to teach me how to live better.

I can tell you that those that passed easiest were those that had faced many fears throughout their lives and had found that somehow they were okay. I believe that facing those fears gave them the peace to face the fear of death and to believe that they will be okay on the other side of this life transition, as well.

I have a ten year old. I repeat as a mother the same things that my parents before me did, in saying that I do not envy my daughters generation, as they have so much more to be afraid of. As the world goes faster, kids are forced to grow up faster. How do we protect our children? How do we teach them all they need to know? Schools pressure us to keep the kids at the top and not let them fail. Society criticizes those that have failed. Sports events support the winners and forget the losers. If we are always acting to never fail, then how to we face that fear and learn the lessons that strengthen us. I have read many stories of those that we would consider "successful", and believe that these people would not be as successful had they not faced the fear of failure and learned from it.

I had several role models in my family for facing fear. My mother died thirty years ago from breast cancer. My memories of my mother are two-fold – she was at times a very active figure in our family and in the community, or she was bed ridden undergoing what would be considered these days barbaric surgeries and treatments. She was diagnosed with the disease in her 30's only a few years after I was born. She was an "old" mom for her day. My parents faced surgery after surgery, treatment after treatment, with four young kids, no health insurance, a self-employed bread winner, during a time where you did not "air your dirty laundry". This continued for nearly twenty years. My parents faced together the fears of caring for the children, losing businesses, losing each other, losing their homes due to bills, you name it. People ask me how they did it – the answer – they had to.

My mother would pull herself through, brush herself off, and start again. The pulling herself through was the " facing the fears part". In some ways my parents were not given some of the skills and help that is out there today for the pulling yourself through. When Mom was going through incredible grief because she lost her sister and mother back-to- back to breast cancer (then lost three children to stillbirth at the same time, probably from the stress) and was having issues with pulling herself up and dusting herself off, the answer society gave was to give her electro-shock treatments. Today, so much more is known to help face these emotions.

The Professional Woman Network has a conference every year that I try to attend as often as possible. I have been coming to the conference on and off over the past fifteen years. My life and perspective of life has changed significantly over the years, much with help from the concepts and ideals promoted by this network. Several years ago, we were given the task of discussing what key element we felt makes us successful. I'm kind of a last-minute person. My mind's always working on the issue, but I never write it down until the last minute. So here it was one hour before our evening meeting and I thought I'd take a bath. So, I'm in the middle of deciding how to get all of me submerged comfortably in a too-short tub, when the key hit me. The key to success was when I accepted in my soul that "I was captain of my own ship". I offer that the concept sounds simple, but is not always easy to execute. Now, I am not saying that we can control or predict what will happen in our life. There is a lot in life that will happen that we cannot control, nor could we have predicted. This is evident in the opening passages of this chapter, where I speak about living with death and the impact of illnesses. I do offer, however, that we have the power over our choices, including if we will be bold enough to face the events and the fears that arise as life happens.

Growing up as a product of these experiences, I can tell you I have had to face my own fears and those that were instilled in me from those times. Our family has many stories in its many chapters. The one I would like to share with you is the story of my awakening. From my experiences, I had become the "over-achiever" in the family. To give you some background, I had always done well in sports, well in school, and somehow always became the leader of groups throughout my youth and schooling years. My mother died my freshman year of college. The last time I spoke to her before she died, she and I had discussed my continuing through college. She saw me as the hope for the family, in that regard. Due to family circumstances, I began living on my own at nineteen.

As we discussed, I completed school on a work-study program, and upon graduating, I began working for the engineering company I had worked with during school. I was the first woman hired by my company that was not a secretary or librarian. At that time, there were 100 employees. The departments fought over who was going to be stuck with "the girl". They didn't want me, especially in construction inspection. Now, to speed it up and skip over fourteen years – I was loyal and worked hard and long, and worked my way up to client manager the way you should, and was at the point of being offered stock and the position of associate in the company. The first woman! I was making a significant living salary-wise, was about to marry a "successful" man – we had a four bedroom house on the water, two boats, motorcycle, 2-3 vacations a year, and my prized possession, my dog Shy. Cinderella revisited. I was a success, or I so I thought….

Then life struck – my older sister, who had suffered with breast cancer on her right side three years prior, was now facing the possibility of it being on her left side. Although tests later revealed it being not a threat at the time, the nature of tissue removed was consistent with that of tissue found in patients with hereditary cancer background.

Science was confirming our belief that the cancer was handed down. When we investigated further into the family, we discovered that the ladies' cancers began mostly in their early thirties, and some in their 20's. I now had three cousins in their 20's who had also been diagnosed. I was at the ripe age of thirty-three, rising in my career and a prime target. (Stress, by the way, being a major trigger). I was approached by my sister's oncologist with the concept of preventative treatment. A first again, as I had the opportunity to be proactive rather than reactive. I chose to be proactive and had a preventative bi-lateral mastectomy and reconstruction. It took a year and three months from decision to completion (note this was thirteen years ago and, although common now, it was revolutionary at the time). That year was terrifying and empowering all at once, and the most significant of my life. I was not happy with the reality. I thought I would lose my femininity. I felt that I would become undesirable. I was choosing to be an amputee. I knew in my heart it was the right choice, but I was full of fear over how this would impact me. I had no idea of the path it would lead me on – a path of empowerment. I was facing my greatest fear – death by cancer – and making a conscious decision for life.

In 2000, I had the honor of being the keynote speaker at the Southwest regional conference for the Society of Woman Engineers. The theme was – "Enrichment of the Mind, Body, and Soul" – pretty revolutionary for a group of engineers. Traditional engineering for many was based in the "work until you drop" ethic. They just want your mind and body; forget what it does for the soul. In many ways, the business concept of a "successful" person was driven by a societal view of monetary stature and achievements.

I want to challenge that view. I suggest that success is less global than that, and is one that is a *personal definition*. I further suggest that success is an ever-changing journey, not a destination. Now, your definition may or may not include those of a traditional societal message. But I would offer the opinion that part of what defines your success would hopefully include terms such as happiness, satisfaction, and fulfillment. Kind of that, "Be all you can be" thinking changed to, "Be all you want to be." The emphasis being on "YOU" – mind, body & soul – a balanced goal for success. I know you are saying that this chapter is about confronting fears – I offer that facing fears and a successful life go hand in hand.

I have learned quite a lot over the past fifteen years about the power of fear. The obvious being from those created from 9/11. Living across from New York harbor, we observed the event, and had family, neighbors and friends killed or nearly killed. We participated as a community to assist those impacted, and to this day have memorials in our towns to always remember our lost members. The fear created from this type of event is very controlling. There are outwardly noticeable impacts from the fear, and inward ones that, I offer, control you even more. Those are the ones that subconsciously guide your reactions and responses to things. These are the ones that sway the choices that you make without you really being aware of it. It is that post traumatic stress syndrome type of fear. These fears can exist from chapters that may not be remembered by us, or even ones that may, as an adult seem trivial, but were huge to us as kids.

I remember hearing that one of the definitions of fear was "False Evidence Appearing Real". Now, we have all experienced real fear associated with real situations. The issue that is being discussed is the fear that controls even after we are removed from the situation. This is where our mind takes scenarios and anticipates them as being possibly ours in the present or the future. Fears that are based on past realities can be helpful to allow for proper planning or precautionary thinking. However, the problem comes in when the fears take over and control our choices beyond precaution and into inaction.

That is when the fears become the driver of our lives. The hardest thing is that many times we may not even understand that this is what is happening to us. Classic cases of post traumatic stress are clear examples of this. Like when a returned veteran dives under a table when he/she hears a commuter helicopter fly overhead in reaction to old war; or when an abused child cowers when someone approaches to give them a hug in reaction to prior beatings; or when a battered woman, removed from the abuser, still feels his influence. In my case, my sisters and I were raised believing that we would be victims, like the other women in the family, and that we would not live past fifty-five years of age.

The beginning of my awakening came after my operation, when I was home alone with myself for 3 months. My best friend, my dog Shy, had passed away four months earlier, my husband worked long hours; I was restricted for a while from driving, so there was a lot of time to think. I discovered I was miserable. I had allowed my "victim" life to invade almost all parts of my life. My choices were made from that position. I discovered that I was run by fears and too afraid to admit it. I was in a constant state of stress and chaos, so I had no time to evaluate life. I appeared strong to outsiders and myself, but cowered within my relationship. I didn't want to see it, I didn't want to admit it, because then I'd have to do something – and I was afraid of being alone.

I also realized that the work environment I had placed myself in was not allowing me to blossom as a person. I'd never been truly out there on my own. I had been with the company since I was a teen. So now that I knew I was miserable, what do I do with it?

Well, of course, the first thing to try is to get everyone else to change. Makes sense. If I can get them all to see what they are doing, then I'm sure they'll change and I can stay where I am. I can stay in my marriage. I can stay in my work environment; all will be fine with the world. I don't have to go out there alone. In essence, what I was choosing to do was to place the power of my happiness in everyone else's hands, and wondering why it wasn't important to them.

I remember reading a book several years ago that has stuck with me. The book was called "*Cinderella Syndrome*" written by Lee Ezell. (It is out of print now). The concept of the book dealt with the notion of women guiding their lives with fairy tale thinking.

More specifically, women respond passively to life's situations, waiting for **others** to make the changes for them. (Kind of like waiting for their prince to come and save them.) I realized I had taken on that role. I needed to face that reality and accept responsibility for my life. By choosing to have the preventative operation, I had faced my greatest fear. This strengthened me to handle these other fears and look at my life objectively. I discovered that, if you can't get your needs met where you are, change something. Either change where you are looking to have them met, change what it is you feel you need, or just change your perspective. Sometimes what we needed it right in front of us, we just thought it would look different.

It is not easy confronting your fears. The following are some pointers to help guide you to the other side:

1. <u>Even if a Prince comes, we are responsible for our own lives.</u> Be an active participant.

2. <u>The hardest part is coming to the point where you realize that something is not right.</u> When this happens, start assessing to whom you are looking to have the situation improve. As women, we have a history as long as humans have roamed the Earth of being the caregivers and giving up ourselves for others. To face our fears and reach our greatest potential, we need to know who we are as individuals and where we have come from. Each of us has our own series of chapters from our gender, to our ethnic background, to the part of the country we come from, the neighborhood, the family, your parents, your siblings, and the chapters from the people we meet along the way. All are influences in our conscious, and more importantly, our subconscious. To unlock our subconscious and discover who we are, and what we really want, we need to peel away at those chapters and understand those influences and values and look into what the fears have locked away inside. It's a hard job, because it means questioning what we have taken for granted.

3. <u>It is important to realize that you cannot go it alone.</u> If we could do it ourselves, we would have changed years ago. It takes other views to see that what we may think in life is not just life for all. If you come from a background where discrimination is the norm, then you may not realize you are being discriminated against.

4.   <u>Be hungry for information.</u> Be willing to open up to other views and perspectives. Also, be willing to talk about the new information. Question everything and work through the feelings it brings up. This is the process of discovering what is right for your views and values. Take the good and come to peace with the bad. I am not saying that this is an easy task. It is a life journey. Your environment may rebel against you searching out different information. This requires that you find a safe nurturing environment within which to do this. This can be in many forms and many places – school, religious facility, therapy, discussion groups, books, friends and family depending on the issue. Some may have supportive environments and some may not. Find the right one for you.

5.   <u>Be willing to reduce/eliminate your escape mechanisms.</u> – Alcohol, drugs, comfort eating, wild relationships, obsessive behavior. You can't face something and escape at the same time. If you truly want to change things, you have to be able to see it clearly. Also, be willing to be around those who do not use these mechanisms so that you can learn the impact of these on your ability to change your life. These may keep you from really looking within.

6.   <u>Be willing to stretch your comfort zone.</u> We do not create changes by being the same. Unfortunately, society tends to punish those who are different. But it is the women who dare to be different that have left the greatest mark. Dare to explore. Sometimes the boldest way you need to be is to be willing to go places where they are willing to do something different. If you are shy, try a speaking class. If you talk all the time, try listening to others. Sometimes it takes years to build up the strength of personality to face the larger

fears. If you keep going, something will eventually change and will rub off. When you change, your situation changes.

7. <u>Remember to celebrate each baby step you may have along the journey.</u> A lot of baby steps will get you places. There will be times that you will be in a place that I call the hall. That is when you have left one area and have not entered the other. Usually, when I am in this place I do not really know what the other side is going to look like. The door has not opened yet. I believe in a gracious Higher Power. I find that when I am open, working on myself, confronting my fears as best I can, stretching my comfort zone, and making decisions from my center, that I go places I would not have dreamed of. When I am not open, doing the same old stuff, making decisions from a place of fear – I go to the same old place – the dark zone. I do not always know when I am in the dark zone. My rule of thumb is to see if it feels like I am hitting my head against the wall and getting nowhere, no matter what it seems like I do. That is when I need most to open myself up by doing something different, until I move past the wall in the hall and to the next door. I have found that volunteering in some way to help others in need works like a miracle to open me up.

8. <u>You don't have to always take things on all at once</u> – I have found that the things I fear most keep hitting me in the face throughout my life. I would beat myself up if I felt that I should have been bolder, or should have done something better. Be kind to yourself. There is always someone out there to criticize you; don't do it to yourself. If you realized you could have done it better, then use it as a learning experience. It will come around again. How do I know this? Well, I have learned that wherever I go, there I am. Any

fears that burp up and do not go all the way away, will have an opportunity to burp up again as it is inside of me. Life is one big lesson. We can learn from anyone, anywhere, at any age.

The summation of my awakening is that I needed to accept deep in my heart that it is <u>my</u> responsibility to strengthen myself to face my fears, ask for what I need, and pursue it.

The risk is that others may not be willing or able to provide it. Then, it is my responsibility to decide to live with the status quo, or venture beyond what is known and comfortable into the unknown to achieve the goal. And what is that goal? The goal is to follow my path taking on what life gives me, keeping me in the process, and to reach my greatest potential.

The ending portion of the story is that each of the three girl siblings in my family has had preventative breast surgery and reconstruction, and preventive hysterectomies. To date, each sister remains cancer free. We have been advised that the studies over the past 15 years of hereditary breast cancer has confirmed that the types of surgeries we had reduce our chances for cancer from 95% to 4%. But even better, by facing the fears along the way, I was able to be strong enough to participate in the very intimate last moments of those that I love. We were able to comfort each other, share memories of our lives, and face the fear of the transition together, with love. When I was a child, my mother's death felt somewhat like our death, too. Now, these experiences have taught me that by sharing their passing, I can learn to live life better, fuller – facing my fears as they come.

Key Point Summary

1. We are responsible for our own lives.

2. Be bold to awaken to your reality.

3. You cannot go it alone.

4. Be hungry for information. Find a safe, nurturing environment in which to do this.

5. Be willing to reduce/eliminate your escape mechanisms – Be willing to be around those who do not use these mechanisms.

6. Be willing to stretch your comfort zone. When you change, your situation changes.

7. Remember to celebrate each baby step you may have along the journey. If you are in a dark place, find your way to open yourself back up.

8. You don't have to always take things on all at once – Life is one big lesson. We can learn from anyone, anywhere, at any age.

ABOUT THE AUTHOR

TERRI TIBBS

Terri Tibbs is a certified trainer and a member of the Professional Woman Network (PWN). Her workshops are designed to provide individuals with the necessary stimuli that motivate them to take action, discover potential, embrace change and seize opportunities.

She has over twenty years experience in the field of Human Resources and holds a Bachelor's degree in Psychology from N.C. A&T State University and a Masters degree in Human Resources Management from S.U.N.Y, Binghamton.

Ms. Tibbs has served on a number of Boards, including The PWN International Advisory Board, Girl Scouts of America (Illinois Crossroads Council), Shepherd's Gate Hospice, TSOD Church Advisory Board and the United Way Allocations.

In addition, to *Women as Leaders*, she has also co-authored *Overcoming The Superwoman Syndrome.*

Contact
(847-543-9380)
Trt731@aol.com

TWENTY-FOUR

UNLOCKING YOUR PAST

By Terri Tibbs

"We delight in the beauty of the butterfly, but rarely admire the changes it has gone through to achieve the beauty." —**Maya Angelou**

We have finally arrived! We've weathered the storm(s) of life. We've bounced back from disappointments and heartaches. We've learned to forgive others and ourselves.

We've overcome many obstacles. We are successful on many levels. *Now What?*

The Journey

Life is like a journey. We set out one day headed for a specific destination, called destiny. We weren't sure how long the trip would take, nor the real cost that would be incurred. We didn't always have clear directions or reliable resources to get us there. We traveled through rain, sleet and snow. At times, we had to pull over or take alternate routes. We missed exits and warning signs on the way. At times, we continued our trip on empty. We picked up riders and experienced peaks and valleys along the way.

Yet, we continued on our trip, determined to get to that place that we knew would hold our destiny.

Some years later, we finally arrive at our destination. This should be a happy and joyful time. Unfortunately, we feel an "emptiness" that won't go away. For many of us, we arrive alone with many regrets and disappointments. The soul mate who promised to never leave us is gone. The loved ones that we sacrificed so much for don't seem to have time for us. Those who have played a significant role in our lives are off trying to find their way.

We have the diplomas, the degrees, the houses, the cars, the careers and the titles. Yet, there remains a big void in our lives. We just don't feel complete. The things that we thought were so important early on don't seem that important anymore. We don't recognize the person that we have become. Somewhere along the way, we lost ourselves.

We've placed our dreams on hold.

We took ownership for problems and issues that were not ours to take.

We blamed ourselves for things that were beyond our control.

We allowed alcohol and drugs to numb our hurt and pain.

We've tried to be all things to all people.

We've carried our hurt so long that it now feels part of who we are.

We've failed to forgive ourselves and others.

It's no wonder that we don't recognize who we have become. We have acted from our place of need on so many occasions. A place that we thought would keep us centered and safe. A place of make believe. If I tell myself that I am okay, then no one will ever realize how well I've learned to mask my inadequacies and fears. If others validate me in some fashion, then maybe I am okay. The problem with this cycle is I am human and may disappoint those that I have come to expect validation from.

When this happens, they may become disappointed and withdrawn in their dealings with me. Leaving me to deal with re-kindled hurt and rejection from my past. Since I am deeply hurt, I fail to realize that they too are acting from their point of need. That place of need may be:

- *The need to be accepted.*

- *The need to be validated.*

- *The need be liked.*

- *The need to be included.*

- *The need to be valued*

- *The need to control*

Can you relate to a time when you acted from a place of need?

If so, what needs were you trying to meet?

_____

Did your actions accomplish your goal?

_____

We need to realize that when we give these things priority in our lives, we are setting ourselves up for rejection. It's a known fact that whatever we give energy to will grow.

Coming To Terms With Where We Are

I am reminded of my 50th birthday. I had planned my whole life up to this point. Once I turned fifty, it was as if I didn't know what else I was supposed to do. I had accomplished much over the years. I had wonderful friends and a family who loved me dearly. I had spent much of my life being super mom and an over-achieving employee.

My daughter was heading off to college and I had recently been promoted into the position of my dreams. Yet, I felt empty. As I pondered my state of mind, it became clear that my life up to this point was about proving my worth to others.

- As a younger adult, *I felt* that I had to go to college because it was expected.

- As a single parent, *I felt* that I had to be super mom.

- As an employee, *I felt* that I had to give 110% to be viewed worthy of upward mobility.

- As a manager, *I felt* that I had to be tough to be taken seriously.

Were there times in your life, when you acted out of a need to prove your worthiness to others? If so, what did it feel like?

_____

_____

_____

It's a sobering thought isn't it? We lose a part of ourselves each time we do this. We have to stop the cycle!

Reflecting on Where we've Been

Someone once said that the past is behind us, the future is ahead of us, and the present is a gift.

What comes to mind when you think of things from your past that have influenced who you've become today?

_____

If we are honest with ourselves, the list might be quite long. The following would most likely appear on many of our lists.

- *Happy Times*

- *Sad Times*

- *Celebrations*

- *Embarrassing Moments*

- *Victorious Moments*

- *Disappointments*

- *Regrets*

Life consists of a series of events. Each event provides us with an opportunity to learn, no matter how difficult that event might be. Through these events, we learn a lot about others, and if we are fortunate, we learn something about ourselves. Viewing the challenges from our past as gifts, versus something negative, can be very powerful. The key is to extract the positives, which is valuable, and discard the negatives.

At the age of twelve, my daughter was asked about one thing that she was thankful for. Her response, "My parents' divorce", floored me. She went on to explain how she felt loved by both of her parents. However, the divorce allowed her the opportunity to travel and see parts of the world that she may never have been able to see. Ten years later, she feels the same way. While divorces are never happy events, she was able to find a positive perspective in it.

I am often reminded of people who lose their jobs, and later say that it was the best thing that happened to them. It's as if they were given a blank sheet of paper to redesign their future. They seized the opportunities and embraced the new place that they found themselves.

In hindsight, what are some past challenges/events that you faced, and now view as a blessing in disguise? Could it be that these blessings in disguise are really part of our destiny?

1. _____

2. _____

3. _____

It would appear that our past holds the key to our present and future. We often struggle with understanding our ***purpose*** and finding our ***passion.*** Our past holds so many answers to who we are. It allows us to understand the legacy of those who have gone before us. Understanding that legacy may provide some insight into some of the decisions we've made, as well as our passion in certain areas. Our past also holds valuable learning from things that we have experienced. Other people can tell us what they think we are good at, but it's up to us to unlock our purpose and passion. Our past holds many answers to where we are going. The key is to figure out how to unlock our past and retrieve the pieces of the puzzle that represents our future.

Keys to Unlocking Our Past

I offer the following tips for tapping into the past, in an effort to determine our purpose and find our passion.

1. **Identify the tasks and activities that you have found fulfilling.** Be honest with yourselves. Focus on the things that you found fulfilling, and not the things that others told you should be fulfilling.

2. **Identify accomplishments from your past that you are proud of.** These usually reflect our skills, strengths and talents.

3. **Identify one thing that you would do today, if money, time, and education were not factors.** Here lays our dreams and the DNA of our passion.

4. **Describe your strengths, weaknesses, likes, dislikes and fears.** This should be a personal and honest assessment of how we see ourselves.

5. **How would others describe you?** This is how others see you. Remember, perception is real. We may not be able to change the perception, but we can change our presentation.

6. **Identify the things that you find boring or uninteresting.** It's okay to admit that you don't enjoy doing things, especially those things that you've pretended to enjoy for years.

7. **Knowing what you know today, given the chance to change the way you have lived your life, what changes, if any, would you make?** This provides a way to deal with the regrets.

8. **Identify the obstacles that are preventing you from doing what you *really* want to do.** There may be specific things like training or money that may be obstacles for you. A major obstacle that is often overlooked is *self*. Many times, we sabotage our dreams with a lack of focus and drive.

If we are absolutely honest with ourselves, these keys will provide the foundation that will enable us to understand our purpose and passion. It's only when we have clarity around purpose and passion that we can embrace the place that we find ourselves.

Embracing the Place That We Find Ourselves

Life is indeed a journey. We are finally finding the courage to discard the baggage from our past. The things that fear has caused us to hold onto from our past are no longer an issue for us. The irony of the matter is that the baggage or residue from that fear remains.

I have a friend who lives alone and very seldom sleeps in her bedroom. She will fall asleep on the couch, or she will sleep in one of her spare bedrooms. No one could understand why she didn't like to sleep in her bedroom. This odd behavior had become acceptable to her. She recently shared a revelation that she had about her bedroom. The furnishings in her bedroom were the same furniture that she had over fifteen years ago during her marriage. She now recognizes that the bedroom with its furniture symbolizes baggage from her past that needed to be discarded.

Is there baggage from your past that you are still attached to which needs to be discarded? (This may include furniture, clothing, people or regret and unforgiveness.)

1. _____

2. _____

3. _____

We have to make sure that we eliminate the residue that our baggage may leave behind.

The residue can and will be problematic, if it is not dealt with appropriately.

The Transformation

Arriving at one's destination in life is not a single event. It is a process of transformation.

As a caterpillar must go through various changes and stages to become a butterfly, we too must go through a transformation process. We can take what we think are shortcuts along the way, however we cannot eliminate the process. It's through this process that we become like a butterfly–a new creature, who has discarded the cocoon of yesterday and finally embraces the new place of destiny. The following things happen on our journey of transformation:

- *We can see clearly who we are and who we want to become.*

- *We begin to give ourselves permission to change the course of our journey.*

- *We begin to like who we are.*

- *We learn that it is okay to say no.*

- *We learn to take better care of our bodies, mind and spirit.*

- *We realize that we cannot save the world or change people.*

- *We stop comparing ourselves to others.*

- *We learn that it is okay to redefine who we are.*

- *We learn to embrace the place that we find ourselves.*

It is truly a joyous and happy time when we can put our past in perspective, embrace our present, and move into our future with passion and purpose, knowing that ***the Best is Yet to Come.***

Notes:

_____

_____

_____

_____

_____

_____

_____

_____

_____

_____

_____

_____

_____

_____

_____

_____

_____

_____

_____

_____

_____

ABOUT THE AUTHOR

SHARON M. HUDSON

Dr. Sharon M. Hudson is a corporate trainer and an Adjunct Professor. She facilitates education and training via face-to-face, blended courses and online. She provides coaching to employees and students to increase their knowledge, competencies, and skills to ensure their marketability in this fast-changing environment.

She has participated in an international exchange of information with a focus on the adult learner with universities and social service organizations in South Africa. She has her own business, Hudson Institute for Excellence, with a focus on Coaching, Diversity and Women's Issues, and Leadership.

Dr. Hudson's formal education includes a Baccalaureate degree in Liberal Arts, a Master of Arts degree in Communication, Governors State University, and a Doctorate in Adult Continuing Education, Northern Illinois University.

She is a member of Professional Woman Network, National Association of Female Executives, and Federally Employed Women.

She is co-author of *Survival Skills for the African-American Woman.*

Contact
Dr. Sharon M. Hudson
Hudson Institute for Excellence
15774 S. LaGrange Road #250
Orland Park, IL 60462
(708) 227-3737
sharon@hudsoninstitute4excellence.com
www.hudsoninstitute4excellence.com
www.protrain.net

TWENTY-FIVE

LEADING BY EXAMPLE

By Dr. Sharon M. Hudson

It's a clear day. Everything is in order for lift off. Space Shuttle Endeavour has just launched. It's mission: to reach the International Space Station.

Think about the power and speed needed to launch a spacecraft. Think about the calculations and the many processes that had to be identified, developed, and implemented to guide the spacecraft on a particular path into orbit, navigate while in orbit, and be directed back to Earth.

The following gives you an idea of the concerns that must be addressed to launch a space shuttle into flight. Besides these examples, there are hundreds of other considerations that must be addressed.

1. Knowing how weather affects a space shuttle.

2. Someone in that spacecraft needs to know how to land it.

3. Space shuttle inspection methods need to be in place.

4. Technical and communications processes must be in place.

5. The astronauts have to be able to identify and repair damage to the space shuttle while in flight.

6. The spacesuits have to be prepared carefully on Earth before they are packed up for the flight.

7. Something near and dear to everyone, what do the astronauts eat while in space?

How long did it take to put the pieces together to make the mission successful? Was it a stop-and-go process, or did everyone work together as a team continuously to accomplish their goal?

Now let's bring it back home. Without leaving Earth, put yourself in this scenario.

You're sitting behind the steering wheel of a sports car (whichever one you want) with 1160 horsepower, capable of going 134 mph in 1/8 of a mile in 5.29 seconds. You're on a racetrack and your mission, winning the race, is the only option. How do you prepare to lead the pack? What do you do to ensure that the vehicle and you are prepared for the race? How much time would it take you to prepare? Are you going to work on your project for a few days, stop for three or four days, and then get back to it? Don't forget, you want to lead.

Leading and Leadership

What is leading and leadership? The dictionary defines lead as *"to guide on a way; to direct the operations, activity, or performance of."*

When you hear the word "leader", what does this mean to you?

_____

Based on your perspective, what does a leader do?

1. _____

2. _____

3. _____

What would you say are some of the characteristics, or qualities of a leader?

1. _____

2. _____

3. _____

Who would you categorize as a good/great leader? Why?

1. _____

2. _____

3. _____

Are you a great leader? If so, in what way?

1. _____

2. _____

3. _____

What is a leader? A leader is able to set a path, and can motivate and inspire others to follow that path. Before you can get someone to follow a path you set, you have to follow one. The path can be positive or negative. It is your choice.

A leader is not satisfied with settling for the status quo. Whatever their successes are, they still seek something more. They do not procrastinate, but take action when needed.

They listen to others.

You may not have a formal title of leader, but that doesn't mean you're not a leader. Think about it. As a woman, we take on many roles, some of which require leadership skills. These roles include daughter, wife, mother, financial manager, chef, nurse, counselor, teacher, student, employee, boss, housekeeper, project manager, event planner, and business owner. What does leadership entail?

Leadership – is simply carrying out the role of a leader. It is people-oriented, supportive, but not a job title. One of the aspects of leadership involves knowing who you are, discovering yourself.

Self-Discovery

"You can out-distance that which is running after you,
but not what is inside of you."
—Rwandan Proverb

Do you have a microscope or magnifying glass? To lead by example, you must examine yourself first. To look closely at yourself and see who you *really are* can be scary. Be honest in your search of self. Appreciate who you are, but be very honest about what you see.

We're going to start on the road to self-discovery. You need to know about yourself so that you can be a positive example for others. In your search for discovering who you are, it is critical you realize that you have to like and love yourself.

How you feel about yourself affects how you treat yourself and others, how you think, how you view the world and your approach to life, how you go about achieving your goals, and determines the options available to you.

"Self-criticism is a sure sign of maturity – and the first step
toward eliminating any personal weakness." —M. L. King Jr.

Self-discovery is knowing what you stand for and what you won't tolerate.

What are you passionate about?

1. _____

2. _____

3. _____

What injustices in life make you angry?

1. _____

2. _____

3. _____

Fear – An unpleasant, often strong emotion caused by the expectation or awareness of danger; anxious concern. Be mindful of your fears because they can rob you of your potential.

Spiritually, physically, emotionally, socially, financially, what do you fear?

1. _____

2. _____

3. _____

In what ways can you overcome that fear?

1. _____

2. _____

3. _____

Self-discovery is establishing your vision and goals, identifying your values and morals, knowing what motivates you, and what you stand for.

Vision – Where do you see yourself in future years? Look ahead as far as you can.

> *"Life consists in what a man is thinking of all day."*
> —Ralph Waldo Emerson

In your lifetime, what do you want to accomplish?

1. _____

2. _____

3. _____

Goals – What do you want to accomplish? Add one goal to each of the following areas in your life:

- Spiritual _____

- Family and home _____

- Physical _____

- Educational _____

- Career _____

- Financial _____

- Social_____

- Mental and emotional _____

"The difference between a goal and a dream is the written word."
—Gene Donohue

Consider the goals you have listed. Choose three goals and consider how you will achieve those goals.

1. _____

2. _____

3. _____

Develop a timeline and schedule for action to complete your goals.

In three months I need to complete:
In six months I need to complete:
In nine months I need to complete:

In one year I need to complete:

Values – are what you consider important, worthwhile, your highest priority. Knowing these is important because your values impact your life. Here are some examples of values: ambition, integrity, loyalty, credibility, honesty, excellence, dignity, courage, innovativeness, challenge, dependability, generosity, wisdom, optimism, discipline, accomplishment, security, and independence, family, friendship, punctuality, open communication, love and kindness.

List your three most important values:

1. _____

2. _____

3. _____

Do you currently work in a work environment (or are in a relationship) that compromises your values? In what way?

1. _____

2. _____

3. _____

Morals – deal with the principles of right and wrong in behavior, ethics, expressing or teaching a conception of right behavior, conforming to a standard of right behavior, capable of right and wrong action. This is truly a code of behavior. Consider whether your morals and your values are in sync.

List three morals that you live:

1. _____

2. _____

3. _____

If one word could describe what you stand for, what would it be?

_____

Self-discovery also means taking the time to reach into yourself.

1. Set aside some quiet time to listen to your thoughts.

2. Discover your talents (if not known already). Identify what you're passionate about.

3. Define what success means to you (not based on someone else's definition).

4. Identify and remove any negative behavior that blocks your potential.

5. Identify and understand your emotions and what prompts them.

6. Remove yourself from your comfort zone (this enhances individual growth).

7. Realize and understand that it's not all about you.

And on your journey:

1. Expect good things from life.

2. Expect the best from yourself and others.

3. Take care of yourself spiritually, physically, emotionally, socially, and financially.

4. Believe in yourself.

5. Embrace change.

6. Focus on changing certain behaviors for the better.

7. Learn new things.

8. Celebrate achievements.

9. Once identified, turn your weaknesses into strengths.

Leading By Example.

Do you project a particular image when you are around corporate executives and chiefs, and a less favorable image to those you may think are lesser? If so, you need to check yourself. Make a decision on whether you're going to be an authentic person or a phony. Treat people on all levels equally.

"To thine own self be true, and it must follow, as the night the day, there canst not then be false to any man."—William Shakespeare

Your actions and words should say the same thing. This is how you communicate to the world. Because communication is an integral part of everything you do, you should be consistent. Depending on the situation, leading by example will make you an unpopular person. Can you stand up to this? This is where courage comes in. Demonstrating and holding to what is right is sometimes frowned upon and creates ill feelings.

Standing on what is right, even when others attack you, will let your light shine. Guess what, someone will notice your light, whether they say anything or not. This can and will make a difference in someone's life.

You have to be prepared for possible confrontation, so let me share my experience:

I was talking with a small group of people when one of them (whom I'll call X) started talking about someone we all knew. It took X approximately 30 seconds to partly defame someone not present. Two of the others fed off of this negativity and immediately jumped in. I interrupted them and asked them if they thought this was right. They all looked at me strangely. No one responded. It was as if an alien stepped in the room; no one knew what to do or say. After a few seconds of silence, I stated that the gossip was not right, and it shouldn't be done. The subject was changed, but I could tell they were really surprised at what I had said and how abruptly the conversation changed.

I did not want to participate in this tongue-lashing. This was my way of letting them know that. I could have just said it's not right to spread gossip about other people. Based on past experience, I knew that statement would not have hit home. I needed to let them know I did not want to hear it.

Another situation that will make you unpopular is not conforming. Most people expect you to follow the crowd. I enjoy going in the opposite direction sometimes.

> *"Whenever you find yourself on the side of the majority,*
> *it's time to pause and reflect."* —Mark Twain

Leading by example is a continuous process. It is not something you stop doing and pick back up later. It is not a game. How do you demonstrate your greatness? You do this by:

- Taking charge of your life (set the direction to lead yourself)

- Showing evidence of the spiritual qualities

- Being aware of how you treat yourself and others

- Developing and maintaining a positive attitude and self-confidence

- Demonstrating behaviors that are aligned with your values, morals

- Listening

- Taking responsibility for yourself

- Motivating yourself to achieve your goals

- Standing on the truth

- Realizing and understanding you will make mistakes (this is ok, you learn from mistakes)

- Helping others

- Building others (help them achieve their goals, continuously encourage and support them)

- Demonstrating perseverance (*"Press on and keep pressing. If you can't fly, run; if you can't run, walk; if you can't walk – CRAWL."* – M. L. King Jr.)

- Teaching others and being a student (*"Intelligence plus character – this is the goal of true education."* – M. L. King Jr.; *"Education is our path to the future. Tomorrow belongs to those that prepare for it today."* – Malcolm X)

- Embrace change (be open to new ideas)

- Show empathy and respect others

- Make wise choices, be decisive

- Not being afraid to take a risk and holding yourself accountable for the outcome

- Practicing what you preach (be an example, do what you suggest others do)

By showing your greatness, others will follow.

Tools to Lead By

I have always been fascinated with cars – driving, repairing, and restoration. I have my own set of tools to use when I am in the repair or restoration mode. The following are tools you can equip yourself with to lead by example. The items in bold print are what you need in your toolkit. In your search of yourself, I'm confident you will add more characteristics to this toolkit.

Tool	What it Represents to Me
Drill	**My connection with God**. With God, I can drill through anything. I can get through it and survive.
Hammer	I can hit away at things that are not morally or ethically right. These things can destroy my **integrity.**
Screws and a screwdriver	To fasten the links between **self-discipline** (leading myself first), **servanthood** (helping others), and **teachability** (keep leading and keep learning).
Wrench	This is a constant turning of my thoughts to visualize my goals, keep them fresh in my mind, and believe I can accomplish them. This represents **vision, focus, and a positive attitude.**
Jack stands	The stands will keep the car off the ground without moving. This represents **character** (my piece of the rock).
Lug wrench	This removes lug nuts from the wheel. This represents **discernment,** which removes unresolved issues.

Vice grips	To get a firm grip on the project, begin work, and show I can carry the ball. This represents **initiative** and **responsibility**.
Pliers	I can also use this tool to get a grip on a problem and eliminate it. This represents **problem solving**.
Ratchet	Allows motion in one direction – forward. This represents **commitment** (taking action) and **competence** (achieving results).

Based on what you do, others will choose to follow you or not. Leading is a big responsibility because, not only does it affect your life, it affects the lives of others.

Whether leading yourself or others, you'll be faced with many challenges. Learning how to handle these challenges comes with experience coupled with the help of a mentor and/or role model.

As a leader, you learn by doing. Information can be shared through various forms of media (print, audio, video, or verbally), but experience is the best teacher. Learning in the form of doing has the greatest impact on your life. You become a competent, capable leader with the right priorities.

Leading is a difficult task. You'll need courage to do what needs to be done when it needs to be done. Others will see your display of courage, and they will be able to follow what you have done. Display courage in the face of opposition. Having courage does not mean you are not afraid. It means you can stand in the face of fear. You have to stand firm in your actions and beliefs.

"If thou faint in the day of adversity, thy strength is small."
—Proverbs 24:10

Do not attempt to soften the difficult situations encountered by sugar coating what's actually going on. This will do you no good. It will cause you to prolong what you need to do. Remember, obstacles are also learning events.

I leave you with this:

1. **You must operate on the principle of fairness**. Treat people with respect, kindness, and compassion. Remember the Golden Rule – treat others as you expect to be treated. Learn to forgive, let go. Be sensitive to the emotions of others. Show you care.

2. **Set your goals, stretch them, but be realistic**. Encourage others to do the same. Do not be too hard on yourself or others when mistakes are made. You have made mistakes and will again. Your continued action will result in success.

3. **Be humble**. Don't ever think you're more important than anyone else. It's what you do that counts. Be honest. Demonstrate integrity in challenging times. Press on.

Just as NASA or a racecar driver have many concerns to be addressed to achieve their goals, so do you. Sit down and develop your plan for your life, and put your team together that will be instrumental in helping you achieve your goals. Work at it continuously. You will get tired at times, but that's okay. It's a "good tired". It's worth it.

Don't give up. Don't let anyone discourage you. Stay away from negativity. And remember always to lead by example.

THE PROFESSIONAL WOMAN NETWORK
Training and Certification on Women's Issues

Linda Ellis Eastman, President & CEO of The Professional Woman Network, has trained and certified over two thousand individuals to start their own consulting/seminar business. Women from such countries as Brazil, Argentina, the Bahamas, Costa Rica, Bermuda, Nigeria, South Africa, Malaysia, and Mexico have attended trainings.

Topics for certification include:
• Diversity & Multiculturalism
• Women's Issues
• Women: A Journey to Wellness
• Save Our Youth
• Teen Image & Social Etiquette
• Leadership & Empowerment Skills for Youth
• Customer Service & Professionalism
• Marketing a Consulting Practice
• Professional Coaching
• Professional Presentation Skills

If you are interested in learning more about becoming certified or about starting your own consulting/seminar business contact:

The Professional Woman Network
P.O. Box 333
Prospect, KY 40059
(502) 566-9900
lindaeastman@prodigy.net
www.prowoman.net

The Professional Woman Network
Book Series

Becoming the Professional Woman
Customer Service & Professionalism for Women
Self-Esteem & Empowerment for Women
The Young Woman's Guide for Personal Success
The Christian Woman's Guide for Personal Success
Survival Skills for the African-American Woman
Overcoming the SuperWoman Syndrome
You're on Stage! Image, Etiquette, Branding & Style
Women's Journey to Wellness: Mind, Body & Spirit
A Woman's Survival Guide for Obstacles, Transition & Change
Women as Leaders: Strategies for Empowerment & Communication

Forthcoming Books:
Beyond the Body: Developing Inner Beauty
The Young Man's Guide for Personal Success
Emotional Wellness for Women Volume I
Emotional Wellness for Women Volume II
Emotional Wellness for Women Volume III
The Baby Boomer's Handbook for Women

These books will be available from the individual contributors, the publisher (www.pwnbooks.com), Amazon.com, and your local bookstore.